MONEY JOBS!

*Training Programs
Run by Banking,
Accounting, Insurance,
and Brokerage Firms—
and How to Get Into Them*

MONEY JOBS!

MARTI PRASHKER & S. PETER VALIUNAS

CROWN PUBLISHERS, INC.   NEW YORK

AUTHORS' NOTE: The information in this book was compiled from a variety of sources. We have made every effort to verify all facts and descriptions, and to ensure that the information is correct and as up-to-date as possible; however, changes may occur at any time. Any inaccuracies are inadvertent and any necessary corrections will be made in future editions.

Drawing by Stan Hunt © 1983
  The *New Yorker* Magazine, Inc.
Drawing by Booth copyright © 1983 by
  George Booth.

Published by Crown Publishers, Inc., One Park Avenue, New York, New York 10016, and simultaneously in Canada by General Publishing Company Limited
Manufactured in the United States of America
Library of Congress Cataloging in Publication Data
Prashker, Marti.
  Money jobs!
Bibliography: p.
1. Bank employees—Training of—Handbooks, manuals, etc. 2. Financial institutions—Employees—Training of—Handbooks, manuals, etc. I. Valiunas, S. Peter. II. Title.
HG1615.7.T7P73 1984   331.25′92   84-12675
ISBN 0-517-55548-4

10 9 8 7 6 5 4 3 2

Book Design: Rhea Braunstein

To everyone looking for a money job—
we wish you the best of luck!

Contents

Acknowledgments

Our thanks extend to many people: to Barbara Grossman, our editor, who was good enough to take a chance and to David Groff, her assistant, for all his help; to Lucy, for her inspired legal advice; to Bo, for remaining in good humor always; to our research assistants Helen Kauder, Debi Martin, and Jim Mulryan; to Poletti Freidin, for providing us with wonderful working facilities; to Bank of America, for getting us interested in the subject; to our family members and friends for putting up with not seeing us for six months and, in many cases, for seeing us but putting up with us anyway; to Tufts University, Boston University, Harvard University, and Columbia University, for their generosity in letting us use their facilities; and to everyone else who gave us a name, spoke to us, or helped us in any other way. Thank you all— we couldn't have done it alone.

Introduction

Willard Butcher, Chairman of the Board–Chase Manhattan Bank; Roger E. Birk, Chairman and CEO–Merrill Lynch; Mary Cunningham, Management Consultant; George Ball, Chief Executive Officer–Pru-Bache: how did these executives begin their successful careers? In money jobs. What are money jobs? They are positions in entry-level training programs in commercial and investment banks, accounting firms, insurance companies, and diversified financial institutions. Money jobs are the plum jobs—they mean training, prestige, and contacts, *and* they mean big salaries. This book can help you land a money job. If used properly, it will save you time and energy and help you start your professional life on the right track.

Two years ago we were part of the legions of college and business school graduates pounding the pavement in search of money jobs. The information in this book encompasses everything that we now realize would have been useful to us then but that had never before been compiled in one place. *Money Jobs!* provides you with the opportunity to take advantage of the fruits of our labor.

Money Jobs! is a directory, an adviser, and a mentor. Here for the first time is a compilation of this country's choicest financial training programs complete with all the vital statistics you need—including salary ranges, educational prerequisites, interview tips, and individual program descriptions—to find and land a money job.

Money Jobs! will also show you how to prepare yourself through coursework for the job search, how to use your own network of contacts, how to write better résumés, and how to perform well in interviews. Our greatest hope is that it will help you avoid—or at least learn from—the enormous embarrassment and humiliation that can be an integral part of finding a money job.

HOW WE DID IT

The comprehensive listings in this book are based on information we obtained from over 200 trainees and recruiters. We conducted face-to-face interviews, spent hours on the phone, and mailed out countless pieces of correspondence. All the information in *Money Jobs!* comes straight from people who have been through training programs or who work in money jobs.

In cases where certain information was unavailable—because trainees could not be identified, training brochures didn't exist, and/or the company felt the information was proprietary—we have simply included the companies without that information in the listings in Chapters 4 through 8. Also, keep in mind that some institutions may offer more training programs than have been described. All information regarding the size and operations of a company are based on year-end 1983 statistics. Salary information is subject to change. In addition, if we don't list a salary, take a look at other similar companies in the same city—there's often a close correlation.

HOW TO USE THIS BOOK

Are you cut out for a money job? It's important to decide up front whether you can make the required commitment in time and effort. Many trainees out there aren't very happy because the job they got turned out to be different from what they expected. In Chapter 1, we'll describe what money jobs are and we'll help you figure out whether one would be right for you.

Chapters 2 and 3 contain the collective wisdom of all the

recruiters, trainees, and trainers we spoke to on how to get a money job. We talk about classwork, we talk about résumés, we even talk about lunch. Our goal is to provide you with job-hunting tips that are fairly specific to the financial services industry. We think you'll find the information helpful—we certainly would have.

Chapters 4 through 8 are structured to help you get a job in an industry, and at a company, where you will enjoy working. These chapters provide an overview of the five basic kinds of financial institutions—commercial banking, investment banking, accounting, diversified financial institutions, and insurance. They'll tell you what's going on in the industry and where the entry-level jobs are.

The Glossary is designed to acquaint you with industry buzzwords—expressions that you'll encounter in glossy recruiting brochures or during interviews. The first time each buzzword appears in *Money Jobs!* it is marked by an asterisk (*) directing you to its definition in the Glossary. It is important that you know what all these words mean. One of the authors is still convinced that she lost a job at an investment bank after confessing during an interview that she didn't know what M&A* meant!

Money Jobs! will give you a feel for the financial services industry and information on specific opportunities in various companies, as well as tips on good preparation and job hunting. So come on, all you future George Balls and Mary Cunninghams of the world. Dust off your typewriter, treat yourself to some power clothes, and get started finding yourself a money job!

Part I /

PREPARATION

"What do they mean our training program is outdated? We all went through it!"

1 / Is a Money Job for You?

THE CHANGING YOUTH CULTURE—OR, POVERTY BREEDS PRACTICALITY

Fifteen years ago, at the close of the 1960s, a book entitled *Money Jobs!* would have been laughed at, ridiculed, or worse yet burned, right along with draft cards and bras. The book might have been every parent's favorite stocking stuffer for a college-age son or daughter, but would anyone have actually read it? We don't think so.

Well, things have changed. Jerry Rubin, a 1960s student radical, is now working on Wall Street selling investment advice. Flower children have gone the way of the dinosaur, along with the conviction that joining the corporate culture is tantamount to child molesting. Today, college and business school graduates are cutting their hair, buying their first suits, and scrambling to find a job. Ideals that seemed so important to young people in the 1960s have been replaced with the more traditional American values of work and family. Hippies have been replaced by Yuppies.

What brought on this dramatic transformation? Quite simply, the most severe economic conditions since the Great Depression of the 1930s. Over the past few years, the malaise of American industry and the superiority of the Japanese business style have been documented by newspapers and television programs across the country. It seems that our friends overseas recognized that they could manufacture the same

3

products as their counterparts in the United States, only they could offer better quality *and* a cheaper price. Ultimately, American manufacturers in many key industries, such as steel and automobiles, were forced to cut production, lay off workers, and lose money. In the big picture, measures of gross national product (GNP), capital formation, and employment sagged.

For those of us who were in school at the time, the recession proved to be a sobering experience. Many of the companies that had for years visited college campuses in search of potential employees began to cancel appointments; worse, some failed to show up when expected. Those that did visit were hiring only a handful of trainees, or none at all. The hardest hit were the manufacturing firms, which cut their recruiting to a bare minimum. Even the oil companies, such as Exxon and Mobil, were feeling the pinch. News of recruiting cutbacks created panic among many graduating seniors who were suddenly faced with the harsh reality of leaving school without a job, or even the prospect of one.

Most experts agree that the worst of our economic woes is behind us now, at least for the time being. Recent improvements, however, do not necessarily mean that the job market, which has been depressed for the past few years, will suddenly blossom. Rather, progress will occur gradually. During this period, we will all have the opportunity to consider what the future holds for the U.S. economy and, more important, how we can best be in a position to take advantage of it. *Money Jobs!* is here to make that task easier for us all.

WHERE THE JOBS WILL BE

There is no doubt that the composition of the work force in America will change dramatically within the next decade. In an attempt to recapture its once-prominent position in the world economy, the manufacturing sector will be forced to cut down on overhead expenses—in other words, on people. The high-technology industry has been hailed as the economy's version of penicillin, and there are a number of dynamic growth companies that offer attractive opportunities. Job se-

4

curity, however, is most definitely not one of this field's stronger attributes. Warner Communications, a high flier of 1981 and 1982, laid off a whopping 50 percent of its Atari division staff and fired 33 percent of its New York headquarters staff. Smaller companies like Osborne Computer and Victor Technologies either have already filed for protection under the bankruptcy code or are preparing to do so. Competition among producers is high, and today's winners could very well be tomorrow's losers. In general, entry-level positions in this industry are not for the faint of heart.

Where, then, will the jobs be? The U.S. Labor Department has projected that 20 million new jobs will be created in the 1980s, 15.5 million of them in the service industries. Banks, brokerage houses, accounting firms, and diversified financial institutions make up a significant part of this sector. Indeed, the accounting profession is anticipated to be the second fastest-growing market for college graduates.

One definite advantage of the financial services field is its relative immunity to economic downturns. No matter what the state of the nation's present finances, there is always a demand for the types of products offered in the industry— sales and purchases of stocks* and bonds,* bank credit, accounting services, and investment advice. The 1981–1982 recession was a perfect example of this phenomenon. Investment banks, commercial banks, brokerage houses, and accountants all made record earnings by financing and/or advising the parties involved in some of the largest mergers and acquisitions in history. When the board chairmen of Mobil and Du Pont were fighting over Conoco, both called in their investment bankers. When the final papers were signed in Du Pont's favor, the Conoco shareholders made out almost (but not quite) as well as First Boston, the investment bank advising Du Pont.

Regardless of the relative health of our economy, insurers are still collecting premiums and investing them, brokers are still buying and selling stocks and options,* and of course accountants are still performing audits and attempting to reduce corporate tax bills. Many of the sharpest minds in the business community have recognized the attractions of the financial services industry. Sears Roebuck, historically the largest retailer of general merchandise, has in recent years purchased Allstate (insurance), Coldwell Banker (real estate), and Dean Witter Reynolds (securities brokerage). In 1982, 58 percent of Sears's income came from these subsidiaries. Recently, too, Prudential Insurance purchased Bache Halsey Stuart & Shields (investment banking). Both Sears and Prudential, which are now referred to as "financial supermarkets," see the financial services field as a growth area, one in which earnings can be shielded from the effects of economic cycles. To paraphrase one commodities trader, "It doesn't matter whether our clients win or lose, we still get the commissions!"

WHERE YOU FIT IN

Qualifications

One of the primary attractions of a money job is that the employee is essentially paid to learn. As a recent college or business school graduate with limited working experience, you should give primary consideration to the training available in your first position. Remember, unless you have had two or three years of work experience before graduate school, you are basically an unknown quantity. Although prospective employers may have access to your transcripts, they know that, in reality, the relationship between schoolwork and actual on-the-job performance is somewhat tenuous. Training programs open doors by giving you a solid background in a particular field and establishing your credibility in the business world.

In addition, there is no better background for applying to business school than two or three years of work experience at an established financial institution. In recent years, business schools have shied away from admitting students directly from college for fear that, without work experience, these students would not be able to benefit from the MBA course of study. The Columbia University Graduate School of Business, for example, reports that only 20 percent of its student body comes straight from college. Admissions officers are usually very familiar with the various training programs and look favorably on candidates who have completed them. The knowledge and maturity gained during your work experience will enable you to benefit more fully from an advanced business education.

Among college students, one of the most widespread misconceptions about money jobs is that they require a background in accounting and finance. This is simply not true. It is always helpful to have two or three courses in accounting and business, but it is not an absolute necessity. Corporate trainers recognize that it is much easier to teach people the intricacies of financial markets than it is to instruct them in proper English. In fact, strong analytical skills and communications skills, rather than a business background, top the list of qualifications for BA applicants. Among BA trainees in our own program, for instance, majors ran the gamut from accounting to Victorian literature. There is no perfect profile for a money job applicant. Anyone who is intelligent and analytical and who communicates well can qualify.

Contrary to popular belief, you do not need connections to land a position in a training program. Although it does help to be the chairman's daughter, it is not an absolute necessity. People who hold money jobs have almost always obtained them through merit. Connections can be very helpful, however, in establishing initial contact and getting a first interview. As discussed in detail in Chapter 2, successfully using your network of friends and acquaintances is a skill in itself.

On the Job

OK. Let's assume you have an offer for a money job. What should you expect? The majority of training programs are designed to transform people with little or no experience in a given field into productive employees in a matter of months. The type of training required differs for BAs and for MBAs, and each financial institution designs its own program to best suit its specific needs. In general, however, all training programs have one thing in common: they are quite demanding.

The classroom work is often intensive and difficult. Homework assignments are always time-consuming and sometimes tedious, and often require teamwork. The atmosphere may be tense and competitive. On the positive side, the company will be pulling for you. It is not in the best interests of any employer to have trainees drop out of expensive and time-consuming training programs. Because of the scope of their investment, employers are usually eager to support their trainees in every way possible.

You will meet a number of people in your new job. Among your fellow trainees will undoubtedly be individuals with whom you may have interests in common outside of work. The close personal relationships you form with peers will make it easier for you to adjust to your new surroundings.

In addition to developing friendships, you will make important business contacts. As a trainee, you will have the opportunity to impress middle- and even senior-level management in your own firm as well as in client corporations. These relationships can help enhance performance on the job, as well as your understanding of how the business community functions. In addition, if you are particularly impressive in a business meeting, you may be invited to join a client organization. Few other jobs offer the individual this kind of exposure.

Money jobs may be particularly attractive for those wishing to live and work abroad. After one or two years of experience in the home office, many commercial banks will send employees, particularly those with language skills, to work in an overseas office. An assignment abroad is a sign that your company thinks very highly of your performance as well as your ability to take on increased responsibilities. For both college and business school graduates seeking salaried overseas work experience, a money job may be the best bet.

There are a number of tangible incentives for pursuing a money job. Although some very attractive offers are waiting for specifically qualified college graduates—petrochemical engineers, for instance—money jobs offer some of the richest starting salaries on a consistent basis to both BAs and MBAs. Trainee salaries begin at approximately $15,000 to $28,000 for BAs and $25,000 to $60,000 for MBAs. The variation depends on geographic location. In most organizations, the fringe benefits are generous and may include profit sharing, year-end bonuses, special loan and mortgage rates, medical and dental coverage, and pension plans. Some organizations will even pay for MBA programs for their BA trainees.

Finally, there are two critical requirements of any money job: self-confidence and perseverance. Looking for a job can be a trying experience, and before you begin your search it is wise to be mentally prepared for the worst. Don't be surprised to find many rejection letters in your mailbox—just remember that they make good wallpaper.

2 / Preparing for the Search

Finding a job may, in itself, be one of the toughest jobs you'll ever have. Of course, there will always be people who, without seeming to lift a finger, get ten job offers, all in the field of their choice. But they are the exception rather than the rule. For most of us, job hunting is a long-drawn-out, frustrating, and sometimes downright demoralizing experience. Perhaps the worst part of the process is being passed over for a job you know you can do just as well as, if not better than, the next guy. Many times you will be rejected for seemingly uncontrollable reasons—for instance, because of intense competition or someone else's high-powered connections. In this situation, the best course of action is to just keep on trucking. As any book on careers or job hunting will tell you, finding a suitable position requires a proactive, rather than a reactive stance. Know what you're in for before you get knocked to your knees.

Below are a few pointers from our own experiences and from suggestions made by specialists in the recruiting and hiring business. Some of the advice may be more applicable to BAs than to MBAs. After all, you MBAs are supposed to know a few tricks already! We recommend that you use this information in conjunction with the references listed at the end of this book. Always keep in mind that the key to getting a money job is preparation. Know what you want and go for it.

SCHOOL ACTIVITIES

It is a mistake to wait until after college or business school graduation to start thinking about a job. First of all, although it may seem like a pain in the neck, it's much easier psychologically to juggle classes and job interviews at the same time than it is to pound the pavement after graduation when your schedule may be less hectic but your confidence is taking a battering in an alien and sometimes lonely environment. The summer before your senior year, try to work out a game plan for the job hunt. Good timing is going to play an extremely important role in your success or failure. Make a schedule for yourself like the one below. Don't wait until senior party week to get started.

While in school you can take a number of steps to improve your chances of getting a money job. After all, when recruiters look at training program candidates, they carefully scrutinize school records. Recruiters may or may not ask to see a copy of your school transcript—it's really a matter of individual company policy. Chances are, though, that they will ask you about your grade point average.

Grades are important, but so is your course of study, as well as your sports, club, and social activities. Don't underestimate the power of these other factors. In an interview for an account officer* training program in a commercial bank, for example, a college senior with a 3.8 grade point average, a retiring personality, and no extracurricular activities may not fare as well as a prospect with a 3.0 average, a vivacious personality, and a leadership position on the intramural basketball team. The financial services industry looks for a wide variety of talents, but people skills are becoming more important in this business every day.

MONEY JOB TIMETABLE

| Summer before (or at the latest first semester) senior year | 1. Get a list of school's alumni for informational interviews. A list is usually available through the career placement office or alumni office. |

11

2. Make a list of anyone you know well or faintly in the financial services industry.

3. Get in touch with personal contacts.

4. Set up informational interviews with alumni.

5. Send letters to companies not interviewing on campus.

Always remember to follow up with a phone call not more than one week after the letter has arrived. Also remember to send thank-you notes after informational interviews.

Second semester, senior year

Interview with companies recruiting on campus and with outside sources obtained through alumni and personal contacts.

Always remember to send thank-you letters the day after each interview. Make sure you know the person's correct title and mailing address. The best way to obtain this information is to ask for a business card at the end of your interview.

Coursework

If you are just graduating from college, remember that a liberal arts major is not a liability. In fact, most recruiters feel that liberal arts majors probably have better communications skills and more knowledge of the world in general than students who major in technical fields. Whether or not this is true, the point is that if you majored in Medieval literature, don't worry about it. Instead, be proud of it, and be ready to discuss why you decided on it.

Regardless of your major, it is a good idea to take at least one course each in economics, accounting, and computers—

the three languages of business. Recruiters like to see applicants who understand the macroeconomic picture (at least as well as Milton Friedman!) and who read the newspapers and keep up on current economic developments. In addition, even though accounting is offered in many training programs, recruiters like to see applicants who have made a preliminary effort to learn the basics on their own. Because of the increasing importance of technology in the workplace, a knowledge of how computers function in the business community is a plus. You don't have to master all the programming languages, but do get a general understanding of computer applications.

Some people may argue that accounting and computers are technical courses and, for this reason, do not belong in a liberal arts curriculum. But as one of our interviewees so succinctly put it, "The Renaissance individual should be able to read and understand *The Wall Street Journal,* not just carry it around like a flag. He or she should be a master of the computer, not a slave to one." The three elective courses we mentioned—accounting, economics, and computers—won't cramp your style, and they will do much to help you later on in your money job search.

If you are a recent college graduate and are still looking for a money job, it's a good idea to attend school part time. This is a perfect opportunity to take that accounting course you passed over in college or any other business-related course that might prove valuable once you do find a job. When a recruiter asks you what you've been doing for the six months since graduation, you can show that you're serious about training and work. In addition, if you perform well in the business course, the professor may become a good resource for you.

Clubs

Because the financial services industry is becoming so people-oriented, recruiters will be searching for people with an ability to interact with peers. One good way of honing your "interpersonal skills" is to join a club at school. It isn't necessary to be a member of the Young Entrepreneurs Club. A few years of working on the social committee or the school newspaper may look extremely good to an interviewer, particularly if it is in a leadership capacity. Being elected to a leadership position by your peers is very attractive to recruiters because it shows that others have enough respect and trust in you to choose you as their representative. A good way to make connections for the future is to join a club charged with bringing in various luminaries from the business world to address the student body. We have heard of people getting jobs by favorably impressing presidents and chief executive officers of companies during lunch on "Career Day."

If your interest lies in the brokerage business, volunteer to raise funds for your school. Most colleges and universities have annual or semiannual drives during which they hit the phones and call alumni, parents—anyone—in an attempt to raise money. When brokers first start out, they spend all their time on the phone soliciting business. Participating in similar activities at school can help you determine whether you're cut out for this type of career. Fundraising work should definitely be mentioned on a résumé, and so should the amount of money you were responsible for bringing in (except if it was very little).

Sports

Never underestimate the power of being a jock. Recruiters are often particularly interested in successful athletes. In addition to teamwork, which is vital in the business world, there are a number of characteristics good athletes have that may make them good performers on the job. These attributes include the competitive edge, the ability to make tough decisions under pressure, and self-discipline. Of course, you can be a total klutz and still have all these qualifications. The point here is simply that if you are an athlete, don't hide it; the recruiter will probably be favorably impressed. Even if you're not on a school team, try to fit your sports involvement somewhere on the résumé. If you run marathons, for instance, you should definitely say so.

CAREER PLACEMENT OFFICES

Two words of advice about career placement offices: *use them.* Go to career seminars, get yourself videotaped, and have a personal consultation with the head of the placement office if possible. Make yourself known to these people, because they may just look to you when that employer calls up with the one extra slot that has to be filled by tomorrow. Don't be lax about getting yourself on interview schedules, even if it involves pushing and shoving to the sign-up sheets.

If you want a money job, make it a point to take part in the structured recruiting program at your college or business school. If you don't, you may have a hard time later because recruiters may consider it disorganized and lazy of you not to have made the effort to interview on campus. Even if you can't get the interviews with the companies you want, go to other interviews. The more experience you get, the better. Make sure you check the placement office regularly for new listings.

Most schools have a lottery or point system for interviewing. Students are given a limited number of interviews or points, and they have to decide which companies are worth "using up points." For this reason, it is a good idea to see how many interviews you can arrange through your own means first without having to use your point allotment.

This brings us to our next point. Use placement offices but don't lean too heavily on them. For firms that do not recruit on campus, particularly investment banks and smaller companies, you should be acting on your own.

PERSONAL CONTACTS

As with most fields, the financial services industry is a very close-knit community. In today's competitive environment, where recruiters often look at 200 applicants for one position, personal contacts are more valuable than ever. This is particularly true of investment banking firms, which often do not launch major recruiting campaigns. Some firms even require a personal reference from inside the organization before they will grant an interview. So before you begin writing letters to companies, make a list of everybody you know (well or faintly) in the financial services industry. Also find out if your school can provide you with a list of alumni and their current places of employment. These people may be willing to help you, and at the very least they should be open to talking with you about their companies and what their own jobs entail.

Try to set up low-key "informational interviews" with alumni and personal contacts. Phone them at least one semester before you graduate and tell them you are interested in a career in banking or accounting or whatever. Then ask if they would be willing to talk to you for an hour or so. You'd be surprised—most people are more than willing, and they find the initiative of the caller very impressive. A word of warning: The informational interview is definitely not an appropriate time for you to get on your knees and beg for a job. Your goal at this point is to gather information and make a good impression. These preliminary discussions can be valuable to you later in your real interviews.

Think hard about your list of contacts. Often people are convinced that they don't know anyone in the business world, but after reflection they realize that they do in fact know quite a few. Don't be misled by the notion that you have to know very high-level people; sometimes middle-management types can be much more helpful. A young woman told us about a well-connected family friend who got her an interview with one of the five executive vice presidents of a major New York bank. The interview seemed to be going along well when, suddenly, the man jumped up to answer a ringing telephone. After hanging up, he apologized to the young woman, saying, "Sorry for the interruption, but I'm trying to buy a savings and loan in Florida today." Obviously, this man was not part of the world of résumés and hungry college graduates. The same woman had much better luck when a friend directed her to an individual at the account officer level at another major bank. The officer, who was in his thirties, told the young woman that she brought back memories of his own frantic struggle to find a job. He turned out to be a great resource.

Once you complete your contact list, use it judiciously. For example, if you want a personal acquaintance to help you make sure that you are very specific about the job you want. A friend of your father's may be very willing to help if he thinks you know what you want and have some direction in life. From his perspective, nothing is worse than a neighbor's wishy-washy son (or daughter). Remember, you're asking your contacts to recommend you for a position with their company—their reputation and credibility are as much on the line as your own. The best way to handle this situation is to say, "I've been looking into the training program at your firm and am interested in joining it." Then, take it from there. Always supply your contacts with a copy of your résumé, no matter how well you may think they know you.

Some people find it morally repugnant to use their own or their parents' connections. Our position is this: Connections help you get a job, not keep it. Once in, you'll be on your own. If you are good, great. If you're bad, you stand the chance of getting fired just like anyone else. No one is going to do you any favors on Judgment Day. So be realistic. If you've got connections, use them. If you don't have any, develop them through friends and school alumni associations.

RÉSUMÉS

What is the purpose of a résumé? It's really twofold: to give recruiters a good idea of your qualifications for the job, and to supply them with information they can use for discussion during an interview. Again we have two words of advice: *one page*. Some schools recommend specific formats, but most stress simply that you keep the résumé as concise as possible. Résumés are subjective, of course—what looks great to one recruiter may get passed over by another. But there are some commonsense rules. A sample résumé and a résumé make-over are included on pages 18 and 19 for your reference. See if you can tell what's wrong with the "before" sample and apply what you have learned to your own résumé. In addition to the "after" sample that can be used as a model for MBAs, we have included one sample résumé for BAs on p. 21.

If you are going to be interviewing for positions in a number of different fields, we recommend that you prepare a

MONEY JOBS MBA "BEFORE" RÉSUMÉ

Susie Slalom
One Mountain Road
Stowe, Vermont 10000
(313) 555-3009

JOB OBJECTIVE:	Position in corporate finance in an investment bank
EDUCATION:	ABC UNIVERSITY, New York, New York Candidate for MBA—Finance, May 1985 GPA: 3.6/4.0 Business Manager, *The ABC Journal*
	DEF UNIVERSITY, New York, New York BA—Economics, May 1983 GPA: 3.0/4.0 Merit Scholar. Arnoff Foundation grant for research in public policy. Three graduate economics courses. Thesis: "The Capital Asset Pricing Model, What Is It?" 1981–1982—Ecole Française Center for French Language Studies, Paris, France. French Ministry of Education grant. Student liaison with faculty. Varsity ski team captain. Co-founder women's luge team.
EXPERIENCE: 7/83–9/83	*Leader,* Green Mountain Cycling Stowe, Vermont. I led five two-week cycling tours through Vermont. Each group had ten people. I made hotel reservations and got campsite permits.
7/82–9/82	*Intern,* Vermont Public Interest Research Group Burlington, Vermont. I wrote a position paper for the group circulated in Vermont legislature entitled *The Economics of Snowmaking on State Property.* I handled mailings for fundraising efforts.
7/81–10/81	*Dishwasher,* Whiskers Stowe, Vermont.
7/80–10/80	*Salesgirl,* Village Ski Shop Stowe, Vermont.
SKILLS:	Fluent in French; computer skills.
OTHER:	Enjoy competitive skiing, cycling, and travel.
	References available on request.

"MAKE OVER"

Full name
no nicknames

(Susie) Slalom
One Mountain Road
Stowe, Vermont 10000
(313) 555-3009

make sure you have a
number where you
can always be reached
or where a message
can be left

optional

JOB OBJECTIVE: Position in corporate finance in an investment bank

EDUCATION: ABC UNIVERSITY, New York, New York
o.k., but what Candidate for MBA—Finance, May 1985
did she accom- GPA: 3.6/4.0
plish? Business Manager, *The ABC Journal*

not good enough to DEF UNIVERSITY, New York, New York
make note of - BA—Economics, May 1983
should be 3.3 or GPA: 3.0/4.0
better Merit Scholar. Arnoff Foundation grant for research
in public policy. Three graduate economics courses.
Too much crunched Thesis: "The Capital Asset Pricing Model, What Is It?"
up together. Segment- 1981–1982—Ecole Française Center for French
ed has more Language Studies, Paris, France. French Ministry of
eye appeal Education grant. Student liaison with faculty. Varsity
ski team captain. Co-founder women's luge team.
elected or appointed?

EXPERIENCE: *should* Leader, Green Mountain Cycling
7/83–9/83 *have more* Stowe, Vermont.
punch I led five two-week cycling tours through Vermont.
Too many words- Each group had ten people. I made hotel reservations
does not fully convey and got campsite permits.
responsibilities

7/82–9/82 *Intern,* Vermont Public Interest Research Group
Burlington, Vermont.
I wrote a position paper for the group circulated in
Too many Vermont legislature entitled *The Economics of*
words, also *Snowmaking on State Property.* I handled mailings
no results for fundraising efforts.

7/81–10/81 *Dishwasher,* Whiskers *We can get rid of*
Stowe, Vermont. *these and still*
show she worked
7/80–10/80 *Salesgirl,* Village Ski Shop *over the summers?*
Stowe, Vermont.

SKILLS: Fluent in French; computer skills *what in*
particular?

OTHER: Enjoy competitive skiing, cycling, and travel.
won any races? achieved anything
References available on request. *unusual?*
optional

19

MONEY JOBS MBA "AFTER" RÉSUMÉ

SUSAN SLALOM
One Mountain Road
Stowe, Vermont 10000
(313) 555-3009

EDUCATION:

ABC UNIVERSITY, New York, New York
Candidate for MBA—Finance, May 1985
GPA: 3.6/4.0
Business Manager, *The ABC Journal*
Increased advertising revenue by 50 percent.

DEF UNIVERSITY, New York, New York
BA—Economics, May 1983
National Merit Scholar. Arnoff Foundation grant for research in public policy. Three graduate economics courses. Thesis: "The Capital Asset Pricing Model, What Is It?"

1981–1982: Ecole Française Center for French Language Studies, Paris, France. French Ministry of Education grant.

Elected student-faculty liaison, 1982–1983
Elected captain, varsity ski team, 1983
Co-founder women's luge team, 1981

Partially financed education through summer work as retail salesperson and restaurant employee.

EXPERIENCE:
Summer 1983

President, Green Mountain Cycling
Stowe, Vermont.
Solely designed, marketed, and led five two-week Vermont tours. Negotiated all accommodations and permit arrangements. Managed finances and itinerary. Selected and guided ten participants per group.

Summer 1982

Intern, Vermont Public Interest Research Group
Burlington, Vermont.
Authored a position paper circulated in Vermont legislature entitled *The Economics of Snowmaking on State Property.* Oversaw fundraising-by-mail campaign. Developed new targeting system which improved returns by 20 percent.

SKILLS:

Fluent in French; proficient in FORTRAN and BASIC.

OTHER:

Competitive cycling: finished Cycle across America race. Enjoy competitive skiing and travel.

References available on request.

MONEY JOBS BA RÉSUMÉ

SUSAN HERMAN
One Statler Avenue
Scranton, New York 10000
(411) 555-1560
(411) 555-7177 (messages)

EDUCATION:

AB UNIVERSITY, Scranton, New York
Candidate for bachelor of arts degree, May 1985.
Major: World Affairs/Chinese
Six courses in economics; two courses in calculus.
Honors: Foreign Policy Workshop, January 1984.
         Dean's List, Spring 1981.
Elected chairman of social committee—administered
$5,000 budget for ten separate campus activities.

THE HIGH SCHOOL, New York, New York
Graduated June 1981.
National Merit Scholar semifinalist.

EXPERIENCE:
Fall 1979

New York City Department of Sanitation
Office of Street Cleaners
New York, New York
Staff Analyst
Compiled performance reports for unit, which were
submitted to senior management and Mayor's office.
Developed new reporting system resulting in 25
percent improvement in streetcleaning efficiency.

Summer 1978

Read-a-Book Company
New York, New York
Publishing Intern
Rotated through divisions, including subsidiary
rights, contracts, marketing, and publicity. Completed
special project to ensure the accuracy of an
economics textbook.

Summer 1976

Carl Marx, Member of Congress
Washington, D.C.
Congressional Intern
Researched and drafted congressman's statement to
committee on food stamps. Prepared press releases
and maintained clippings files.

SPECIAL SKILLS:

Fluent in Mandarin Chinese; working knowledge of
Japanese.

OTHER:

Competitive marathon runner; finished New York
Marathon. Enjoy music, theater, and tennis.

21

separate résumé for each field, stating the appropriate career objective on top. If you are a BA, it isn't necessary to have a career objective. Let's say you are applying to a commercial bank that runs a number of different training programs and you're not quite sure which way you want to go. You might want to leave off the career objective entirely. There's no reason to limit your chances right from the start.

When you format your résumé, remember that different institutions will be looking for different strengths. Your job is to know and stress what might be important to the recruiter. This will be a natural by-product of your research efforts.

If you decide to work up a number of different résumés, make sure you get each one printed separately. Don't try to save money by typing in a professional objective tailored to the company at the receiving end. This usually looks sloppy and is easily detected. Also stay away from long narratives about your job experiences. Highlight achievements and projects, and be as quantitative as possible. For instance, instead of saying "Worked on a project to streamline operations," say "Participated in project to streamline operations which will result in savings of approximately X dollars."

Every word on your résumé should be chosen carefully. Recruiters do not have the time to sift through long-winded copy. Unless they see something striking, chances are they'll just move on to the next résumé. A graduate school of business suggests using words that express action and responsibility in describing your past experiences. We recommend this approach and have included a list of such words below:

ACTION WORDS

accomplished	approved	calculated
accelerated	arbitrated	collected
achieved	arranged	commented
administered	assisted	communicated
allocated	attained	compiled
amended	audited	completed
amplified	augmented	computed
analyzed	awarded	conceived
appointed	broadened	conceptualized

condensed	founded	programmed
conducted	gathered	promoted
consolidated	governed	proposed
constructed	guided	published
contracted	implemented	purchased
contributed	improved	recorded
contrived	increased	recruited
controlled	initiated	rectified
coordinated	issued	reduced
created	installed	regulated
delegated	instituted	reinforced
delivered	interpreted	researched
demonstrated	interviewed	restored
designed	introduced	resulted
determined	invented	revamped
developed	investigated	reviewed
devised	launched	revised
devoted	maintained	scheduled
directed	managed	selected
distributed	marketed	served
documented	moderated	serviced
drafted	modified	strengthened
edited	monitored	studied
elected	negotiated	suggested
eliminated	offered	summarized
enlarged	organized	superseded
established	originated	supervised
evaluated	overhauled	systematized
examined	performed	terminated
executed	planned	traced
expanded	prepared	trained
extended	presented	transferred
forecasted	preserved	translated
formulated	presided	unified
formulized	processed	utilized
fortified	produced	

Have the résumé printed on white bond—no fancy colors, please; they will only be distracting—and proofread it carefully. Needless to say, résumés must be absolutely error-free. Nothing turns a recruiter off more than misspellings or incorrect punctuation.

23

CHECKLISTS

Once your résumé is in reasonably good shape, start making checklists of potential employers. Your school's placement library can be very helpful here. Compile a list of all the organizations at which you want to interview. Make sure you have the name and job title of the recruiter (when available), the address, and the telephone number. One of the reasons we do not include recruiter's names in the listings at the end of Chapters 4 through 8 is the high degree of turnover in the field. If you think your source of information is out of date, check it. Otherwise, you run the risk of addressing correspondence to someone who either has left the company or is working in another department. We don't need to tell you where those letters will end up. If you can't get the recruiter's name from the placement office, call the company and ask directly. If you have a personal contact at an organization, make a note of it on your list. Send out the first set of letters and résumés to your personal contacts and to companies that are not recruiting on campus. If you can get an interview outside of the on-campus recruiting system, you will have more "points" or interviews to allot to the recruiting companies.

Leave space on your checklist for noting action taken and results achieved with each company you are contacting. As your job hunt progresses, the list will essentially become a status report. And if you are sending out letters to a fairly large number of organizations, you will have an efficient tracking system in place.

RESEARCH

One of the most crucial elements in a successful job hunt is good research. It will help you accurately target the firms that you will like and that will like you. In addition, real knowledge about the company will help you make a good impression, both through written correspondence and in interviews.

As part of your research efforts, develop a file on each company that contains (1) the company's annual report, (2) any recruiting pamphlets the company distributes, (3) any articles written about the company in the last year, and (4) a few recent articles on trends in the industry. The job-hunting aids and periodicals indexes listed in the References at the end of the book can help you compile these items.

You can obtain an annual report by simply calling a company's headquarters and requesting one. Remember, though, that if a company is privately held, it will not have such a document. The annual report will help you get a feel for the firm's organization, its corporate culture, and its financial performance. It may also give you some indication of industry trends. Most important, it will tell you how the company perceives *itself* as an institution.

Many companies compile brochures specifically for their recruiting efforts. In addition to the compulsory pictures of employees in a factory somewhere with hardhats on, these pamphlets will usually briefly describe the opportunities available in the organization. Articles in the paper about the company will tell you what people on the outside think about the organization.

COVER LETTERS

When you send your résumé, always attach a personalized cover letter. Many recruiters will simply throw out résumés that arrive without them, on the assumption that an applicant who does not care enough about the job to attach a letter is not the sort of person the organization should be hiring. Try to limit the letter to three paragraphs. The first paragraph should explain why you are writing, and at whose suggestion, or how you found out about the job. If you went to a well-known school, mention it. The second paragraph should explain why you are both interested in and qualified for the position in question. Take something from your résumé that you think specifically applies and discuss it briefly. The third paragraph should state your desire to meet personally with the addressee to discuss your qualifications in more detail. You should also request that the company send you its annual report and any information available about its training program. Mention that you will call in a week to set up a mutually convenient time. Follow-up is more important than the initial letter. A sample cover letter appears on page 26.

December 1, 1984

Jane Smith, Professional Recruiter
Sunnylane BanCorp
15 Sunnylane Plaza
Washington, Oregon 10000

Dear Ms. Smith,

I am a senior at Trinity College and am now in the process of researching job opportunities for next year. I heard about Sunnylane, and your entry-level training program for account officers, through the Trinity career placement office. I am writing to inquire about the possibility of my joining the program.

After careful consideration, I have determined that commercial banking offers good opportunities for someone with my background. While majoring in international relations at Trinity, I supplemented my education by taking two accounting courses, three economics courses, and a course in computer science. In addition, I was business manager of the school newspaper, a position that permitted me to get some experience with finance and management. I feel that my liberal arts background, combined with some technical training and hands-on experience, has prepared me well to successfully pursue a career as a bank lending officer.

I have enclosed my résumé for your information, and I would like to set up an appointment at your convenience to pursue the opportunities available at Sunnylane. I will call in the next week to discuss this possibility with you. If you have an annual report, as well as any printed material describing the training program, I would very much appreciate receiving copies.

I look forward to talking with you.

Sincerely,

Money Bags, Jr.

3 / *The Interview*

HOW TO DRESS

First impressions are based largely on appearance, so make sure you look good. If you want to join the business world, you must dress the part. Keep in mind, however, that you won't get a money job because you dress well; you just won't get one if you *don't* dress well. Because recruiters are usually overwhelmed with applicants, they may look for ways to eliminate you immediately, so leave your sneakers and Wallabees in the closet on interview day. The best thing to do is play it safe. Why feel nervous about what you're wearing when there is so much else to think about at an interview?

Men should wear dark, conservative suits in a fabric appropriate for the season. Don't wear a winter-weight wool suit in the dog days of August. Three-piece suits are no longer de rigueur; two-piece is perfectly acceptable. The best color choice are gray and dark blue, perhaps with a muted pinstripe. Make sure the suit fits—don't wait until the last minute to go rummaging through your roommate's or your father's closet in search of an appropriate outfit. White cotton shirts and a "Brooks Brothers" type tie (either regimental stripes or a foulard pattern) are your best bets. Do not wear suspenders unless you really think you can pull it off. In the business world "braces," as they are called, are a sign of seniority—you don't just wear them, you *earn* them. They may look a little

"I'd just like to say, sir, that I always make a bad first impression."

Drawing by Stan Hunt © 1983
The New Yorker Magazine, Inc.

cocky on a young man (even worse on a young woman!). Make sure your shoes are shined. It may sound a little silly, but some people may look. They should be good-quality shoes, too. Buy or borrow a pair of wing-tip shoes or loafers with tassels on them. Wear a leather belt with a good, shined buckle. Jewelry is definitely out, except for a watch and perhaps a tie bar.

Women too should wear suits in conservative colors. Blouses should be appropriate for daytime—not too low cut or too sheer—and made of either silk (or a good likeness) or cotton. You don't need to wear one of those little ties, but if you feel comfortable with it, go ahead. Wear plain nude stockings, no texture, no colors, no nonsense. Also remember to carry an extra pair with you. There's nothing more disconcerting than running your pantyhose on the way to an interview. Wear medium-heeled pumps of blue, black, or brown (depending on your suit), and make sure you can walk in them. One woman told about returning from lunch with two male interviewers when she caught her heel in a subway grate. While she struggled to extricate the shoe, her two companions continued up the block and noticed her absence only when the traffic light turned red.

Women should keep jewelry simple: A gold chain, a watch, and a pair of small gold earrings are best. The key to dressing for interviews is to look appropriate and comfortable at the same time. It isn't necessary to carry a briefcase, but one of those leather portfolios with a pad of paper is always useful. Who knows? You may want to take a few notes or jot down someone's name.

Make sure you manage a trip to the men's or ladies' room before going into an appointment. The morning paper does have a way of smudging your hands—and you must read the paper before an interview because that will invariably be the day the company makes front-page news. Don't get a haircut the day before an interview, because you'll probably feel self-conscious. Have it cut the previous week.

THE SCREENING INTERVIEW

At the screening interview the recruiter usually sits in a room all day long and sees different candidates every half-hour or so. You're not given that much time to make an impression. After you leave, the recruiter usually has about five minutes to write up his or her thoughts before the next applicant arrives. Thus, one of your most important goals in a screening interview is to establish a personal relationship with the individual across the desk. Don't forget to make eye contact. When you walk in, try to get a feel for the recruiter's personality. Is the recruiter easygoing, or does he or she look like the type who is going to ask nonstop questions for half an hour? It's important to be very flexible in this situation. Every interview will be somewhat different.

From the information you have compiled during your research efforts, develop about fifteen minutes' worth of questions. The subjects can range from the training program itself to job progression, recent developments within the firm, or newsworthy items about the company or the industry. Whatever the topic, try to make your questions original. Avoid what one interviewer called "canned" questions. If you are going to talk about an article in the press, remember that it's not enough to know about the piece; you should also have a well-formulated opinion about it. Just keep in mind who you're talking to. This is not the time to wear your "Save the Whales" button. Be careful about bringing up negative points about the firm. A little tact is required here since some interviewers take these questions better than others. If an interviewer asks, "What do you know about our firm?" think before answering, "I heard you lost $100 million last year, and that you're being sued by the SEC.*"

First interviews are generally not the time to get specific about salary or benefits. These topics should be brought up in the second interview, when the employer has expressed more concrete interest in hiring you.

The interviewer will be looking for something on your résumé that makes you stand out from all other candidates—for instance, perhaps you majored in something offbeat in college or took time off for travel abroad. Be prepared to talk about your experiences and life decisions positively. The interviewer may try to put you on the defensive, but you needn't fall into this trap. Be professional. If someone asks you what you didn't like about your previous job, or a summer job, don't say you hated your boss or the work was boring. Be diplomatic. Badmouthing a former employer is a definite no-no. Try to turn any weakness in your résumé—a time gap, for instance—into a strength. No matter what misdeeds you may have committed, the worst thing to do is slink down into your chair.

Be prepared for certain stock questions. Our favorite is the "strengths and weaknesses" question. If an interviewer asks you what your greatest weaknesses are, be very careful about your answers. You have to say something, but you don't have to tell the whole truth. Try to find weaknesses that you can turn into strengths—your age, for instance. A good answer would be, "Well, I am 21 (52, whatever) and I look young (old, whatever), but I feel that I am mature enough and experienced enough to be successful in the business world." Or you could say, "I am a perfectionist, and sometimes I have problems working with people who aren't, but the end result is that I do a good job and am able to motivate others." We've included a list of some of the most commonly asked interview questions, and a little bit about the psychology behind them, beginning below. We recommend that you practice with a tape recorder. Tape your answers to the questions and then listen to what you have said. This is a great technique for improving your interview style. You can even get a friend to play recruiter.

When Interviewers Ask You	*What They Really Want to Know Is*
Describe yourself. What in your background qualifies you for this job?	Can you take an incredible amount of information, organize it quickly in your head, and present it in a concise and articulate fashion?

When Interviewers Ask You	*What They Really Want to Know Is*
What are your greatest strengths and weaknesses?	Are my perceptions of your strengths and weaknesses the same as yours? (If you have been meek and timid throughout the interview and then describe yourself as a great marketeer, the interviewer will know something's wrong.) How mature are you in dealing with your weaknesses? Can you identify methods for self-improvement?
Where do you want to be five years from now?	What motivates you and what do you want out of life? Are you someone who expects everything to be given to you? (Did you answer in terms of money, title, or job responsibility?)
Why this industry? This firm?	Have you done your homework? Are you analytical? (Stay away from answers like "I've known I wanted to be an actuary since I was two years old.")
Are you an entrepreneur? A team player? Give examples.	Will you be able to adapt to the firm's workstyle? (You can be both, you know.)
How would your peers describe you?	How do you see yourself? Are you a leader or a follower? (If you have been elected to any leadership roles by your peers, now is the time to mention them.)
What makes you think you'll succeed in this business?	Have you correctly identified the skills required to succeed? Can you prove that you have them?

32

When Interviewers Ask You	*What They Really Want to Know Is*
Have you considered pursuing a graduate degree? (for BAs)	Will you leave after a few years?
Why did you go to business school?	Are you analytical? Do you think out big decisions, or just let life lead you around by the nose?
Why did you choose your major?	Same as above.
What do you read?	What makes you tick? What outside interests do you have?
Where else are you interviewing?	How well have you thought out your strategy for finding a job?
How would you compare our firm with others?	Have you done your homework?
How do you feel about traveling or relocating?	How flexible are you? Is there anything in your personal life that cannot legally be asked directly (e.g., Are you married?) that might restrict your flexibility?
Why should we hire you? What do you bring to this job?	How are your selling skills? If you can't sell yourself, how will you be able to sell our products?

THE DAY-LONG INTERVIEW

If you have made a good impression during the screening interview, you may be asked to come to company headquarters for a day-long interview. If you are coming in from out of town, the company will usually pick up the tab. Be sensible here, of course—don't order Iranian caviar from room service. During the day-long interview, you will probably meet with four or five people. You may be asked the same questions

33

over and over again, and you will have to keep your answers as fresh as possible. One of the biggest turnoffs reported by recruiters is being given a pat answer to every question. You should prepare your responses, but they shouldn't sound that way.

Remember that the questions asked in the day-long interview will probably be more specific than those you faced during screening. Most of the time, the interviewer is not looking for a particular answer but just wants to see how you handle the question. In other words, if someone asks you which way interest rates are going to move, don't just say "up"! Remember, there are no absolute right or wrong answers. Make sure that you ask each person interviewing you for a business card. It will come in handy when you sit down later to write thank-you notes.

During the day-long interview, you will probably be taken out to lunch by one of the people interviewing you, often someone relatively junior in the organization. The first test you will be faced with is the drink question. The waiter will come over for a drink order, and you'll be asked to go first as the guest. Do you or don't you? Well, you don't if half a white wine spritzer makes you see stars. If you can handle it, and feel like having a drink, then go ahead. Don't overdo it, though; one is enough. If you usually don't drink, order a soda or a Perrier—you must get something, because if the interviewer is drinking, he or she will feel more comfortable having you as "company."

Don't order the most expensive thing on the menu, but don't order the cheapest either. Stay away from bony fish or lobsters. You'd look pretty silly interviewing for a job wearing a bib. If the maitre d' comes over to announce the specials and you want one of them, don't ask the price—just use your best judgment. Enjoy your meal!

At the end of the day-long interview, you will probably sit down with the personnel officer. At this time, you should ask when you can expect a response. This is also the time to discuss benefits—vacation, health insurance, sick leave, pension plans, profit sharing, moving expenses, and so on.

FOLLOW-UP

Your job search does not end with the interview. Always write a thank-you letter to each of the people you spoke with—on the same day if possible, and at the very latest the next day. This goes for both screening interviews and full-day interviews. Thank-you letters underscore your interest in the organization and show a professional sense of follow-up. Also, many interviewers do not submit their formal feedback to personnel for a few days, so timely follow-up from you may reach them before they appraise you on paper. If you saw a number of people, write each of them a separate, personalized note—just in case they decide to make comparisons. By the way, these notes needn't be typed—you can handwrite them on good white or cream stationery. Make sure you spell people's names correctly and that you have their proper titles. A sample thank-you letter appears on page 36.

If the agreed-upon time elapses without any response, it is not impolite to call. Many organizations will telephone to make an offer and then confirm in writing, but some firms will reply only by mail. One major bank sends mailgrams to the lucky ones and regular letters to the others. If you call and learn that no decision has been made, take this as a sign of encouragement. You are still being considered for the position. If you are offered the position, be sure to get a written confirmation that specifies what job you've been offered and at what starting salary, plus any other points you consider "dealbreakers." It's the "minor details" that can cause headaches later on.

When you do receive an offer, you will usually be expected to respond in two to three weeks, but always ask how long you have. If you have any questions, do not hesitate to contact the company. Once you firmly make up your mind to accept or reject the offer, it is best to notify the organization as soon as possible. If you are still interviewing with other firms and need additional time to decide, ask for it. The company can only say no.

It is accepted practice to notify other firms you are interviewing that you have received an offer. If they are truly

February 1, 1985

Jane Smith, Professional Recruiter
Sunnylane BanCorp
15 Sunnylane Plaza
Washington, Oregon 10000

Dear Ms. Smith,

I would like to thank you for taking the time to talk with me about Sunnylane's training program on Tuesday. I enjoyed our discussion very much, as well as the opportunity to learn more about the bank firsthand.

I continue to be very interested in joining your training program. I found our discussion about the increasing importance of marketing skills in commercial banking particularly relevant. It convinced me more than ever that my experiences as the business manager of the Trinity *Tatler* would make me a productive member of the Sunnylane "team."

Once again, thank you, and I look forward to hearing from you soon.

Sincerely,

Money Bags, Jr.

interested in you, they will be able to arrange an interview on surprisingly short notice. At this stage, though, it is important to act quickly, and in good faith. If you receive more than one offer, you may decide to negotiate for a higher salary or a different benefits package. But never back your prospective employer or yourself into a corner! If you do negotiate, be careful. Unless you are dealing from a position of overwhelming strength, do not push hard. Some companies work within a starting range, particularly for MBAs, but others have a fixed salary that is not open to discussion. Never negotiate on the basis of a spurious second offer. Doing so is unethical and may come back to haunt you.

When you finally decide which offer to accept, inform your new employer by telephone and confirm in writing. Be sure to let the other firms know, promptly and courteously, of your decision. You never know when you may decide to interview again!

CHOOSING A COMPANY

If you receive a number of job offers, you may be faced with a difficult decision. Assuming they are all for basically the same type of job and at the same salary level, how do you decide which firm to join? What are the most important factors to consider?

It's crucial that you have a good sense of the firm's corporate culture and working style. After all, you're not just accepting a job; chances are you're going to be there for a while. Will you like the place? Get along with the people? Feel a part of the organization? These factors will be as important to your overall professional success as will your intelligence, skills, and appearance. Talk to people in the industry about the firm, its people, and the reputation of the department for which you will be working.

Don't fall into the trap of drawing conclusions about a particular firm because of the recruiter's personality. After all, the recruiter is only one person. And as the director of national recruiting for one of the Big Eight accounting firms told us, "There are a lot of weirdos out there." During the day-long interview, you should have a better opportunity to get a feel for the institution and the types of people who work there.

REJECTION LETTERS

Rejection letters—ding letters*, as they are sometimes called —are no fun. After all the work you put in preparing yourself for the job search, receiving the final no in a thin envelope is a real downer. The fact of the matter is that everyone gets them—they are part of the process of finding a money job. So don't let huge piles of rejection letters send you into a fit of depression. Instead, do what students do at the University of Southern California Business School—have a rejection letter party. Rejection letters serve as admission tickets, and prizes are given for the coldest rejection, the most rejections, and the most unusual rejection. Remember, there's comfort in numbers!

Part II

THE MONEY JOBS! DIRECTORY

4 / Commercial Banks

The business of commercial banking used to be relatively simple: taking deposits and making loans. Rumor had it that banks were run by the "3-6-3" theory: Pay 3 percent on deposits, lend them out at 6 percent, and get out on the golf course by 3:00! Unfortunately, for bankers at least, life has gotten much more complicated. The banking industry has undergone a major revolution, and the changes aren't over yet. High inflation, high interest rates, deregulation, and much more demanding customers have transformed banking into an exceedingly complex and competitive industry.

No longer do banks have the luxury of a captive market willing to accept a fixed return; now they have to shop around for customers and offer favorable rates. Spread income—the difference between the rate banks pay for money and the rate at which they lend it out—is no longer as generous as it used to be. And that afternoon golf game is a thing of the past. Today's bankers work at least from 9:00 to 5:00, and often much longer.

HOW BANKS OPERATE

In very simple terms, banks serve as financial middlemen between those with excess funds available to invest, or to hold available for use, and those with borrowing needs. In this sense, commercial banks and investment banks serve similar functions: Both match up borrowers with lenders, or investors. But while investment banks can underwrite*, or purchase, new stock or equity* issues and then resell them to the public, commercial banks cannot. Historically, "banking houses" like the House of Morgan were permitted to perform both underwriting and commercial lending activities. This practice was made illegal in 1933 by the passage of the Glass-Steagall* Act, one of the most significant pieces of banking legislation ever enacted. After the stock market crash in 1929, Congress decided to separate commercial banking activities from investment banking. The legislators in Washington felt that it was inappropriate for commercial banks to be engaged in a "speculative" activity like underwriting when they had a responsibility to ensure the safety of their depositors' funds.

The failure of the Bank of the United States in 1930 was attributed to excessive speculation on the part of its underwriting operation. The question of conflict of interest also arose, because the legislators were worried that a bank with a shaky borrower might sell that debtor's equity issue to an uninformed public, and thus save the loan from default. Because of these sentiments, the House of Morgan and many similar institutions were forced to separate their commercial and investment banking activities. Thus, Morgan Guaranty became the commercial bank and Morgan Stanley the investment bank.

Until very recently, commercial banks have stuck to the business of taking deposits from both corporations and the public and making loans. They made money through the difference, or spread, between the rate they paid for the money —in the form of interest on savings accounts or CDs* (certificates of deposit)—and the rate at which they lent it out. The banks had, in effect, a monopoly on checking and commercial loan activities, and they raked in the profits. When a small company came in requesting 10-year financing for a new factory, banks would take money that cost them 3 percent to obtain and lend it out at perhaps 6 percent—the 3 percent difference was all gravy. Profits went into building extensive and luxurious branch networks, and banks became notorious for the generous benefits they offered employees.

In the last five years, everything has changed. When interest rates began to soar, investors became more and more dissatisfied with the low or nonexistent rate of return they were getting from their passbook savings and checking accounts. Consumers began to pull their money out of the banks and put it in money market* mutual funds or in NOW accounts —the interest-bearing checking-type accounts offered by savings and loan associations (S&Ls) and other thrift institutions. Previously, S&Ls had not been permitted to offer this service, but in 1980 new legislation called the Depository Institutions Deregulation and Monetary Control Act was passed, giving them many of the powers previously permitted only to commercial banks. Traditionally, S&Ls had been in the business of mortgage financing.

As funds began to pour out of the banks, strategists in the industry realized that they could no longer depend on cheap savings account money and free checking account balances for their lending base. At the same time, many were stuck with a portfolio* of mortgages and other long-term loans in which the spread was "underwater"—that is, the banks were paying a higher interest rate for funds than the rate at which they were lending funds out. In addition, loans to major U.S. corporations provided lower and lower earnings as many companies found alternative ways of financing themselves and as the number of banks vying for this shrinking market increased dramatically. Finally, recessions at home and abroad cut further into profits. The brick-and-mortar investment in branch expansion haunted a number of banks as their profits shrank and real estate values fell.

Banking became a business with very little margin for error. As a result, many of the major players in the industry instituted hefty cutbacks in both staff and facilities. In an effort to reduce expenses, banks closed down branches, installed computers and ATMs* (automated teller machines) to replace the traditional teller, and some even restricted teller service to customers who maintained a certain minimum balance in their accounts.

As taking deposits and making loans became less and less profitable, bankers began to develop strategies for the future.

In the past, many banks had prided themselves on providing "all services to all people." Now it was time to refine their product offerings by capitalizing on stronger operations while getting rid of weaker ones. Bankers Trust, for example, decided to drop its consumer branch banking business and sold its retail operations in 1978.

In addition to selling or simply closing down undesirable lines of business, banks began to search for other products to sell to customers at a profit. Many realized that fee-based services like financial consulting, high-technology cash management systems, and foreign exchange trading—which do not necessarily involve the extension of credit—provide opportunities for high-profit, low-risk business. They also help to bolster a bank's ROA,* or return on assets, a measurement often used to analyze bank performance. Since return on assets is equal to earnings divided by the investment (asset) required to achieve that level of earnings, anything that increases earnings without also increasing investment cost improves ROA. Fee-based services do just this, and are therefore very attractive.

Banks also began to look for ways of luring the individual consumer back from money market funds and NOW accounts offered by S&Ls. Deregulation in 1982, called the Garn-St. Germain Depository Institutions Act, enabled them to compete with the savings and loan associations by offering their own interest-bearing checking accounts, although the number of transactions in the accounts are limited. Many banks have also found opportunities in discount brokerage, a service in which the bank acts only as an order taker, not as an underwriter or investment adviser. By offering both securities* and traditional banking services, banks can provide customers with a wide range of financial services, with the added convenience of one-stop shopping and consolidation of investments.

Today, banks are even getting into the consumer goods business. They offer their customers discounts on merchandise ranging from fur coats to television sets. The size of the discount depends on the number of accounts maintained with the bank or the amount charged on a bank-issued credit card.

This is one more attempt on the part of banks to lure back the retail business they lost in prior years.

ORGANIZATION—THE BIG PICTURE

In the United States, banks are usually divided into three categories: money center banks, regional banks, and California banks. The money center banks include those in key financial cities—New York, Boston, and Chicago. The regionals include banks with a stronghold in a particular geographic market area, be it Texas or Ohio. The California banks, though technically regional banks, are usually classified separately by virtue of both their size and the size of the California market.

Under the McFadden Act of 1927, banks are allowed to have branches only within their home state. Technically, this means that banks cannot offer interstate services to their customers. But banks have been able to sidestep the issue and to solicit corporate business nationwide by setting up out-of-state loan production offices (LPOs), which are charged with bringing in corporate business from their operating region. In spite of the McFadden Act, banks are permitted to operate LPOs so long as the *processing* of any loan made or deposit taken is done within the bank's home state. Under the Edge Act of 1919, commercial banks are permitted to set up subsidiary operations outside their home state for the sole purpose of financing international trade and/or investment. Out-of-state consumers can also be reached through credit cards and discount brokerage services.

If a commercial bank or an S&L is in danger of going under and an in-state institution cannot be found to purchase it, an out-of-state bank may be able to. Some banks feel that it makes more sense to expand across state lines by buying up local banks or S&Ls than by setting up LPOs. This is because local banks already have an established relationship with the community. By buying a local institution, banks can essentially purchase a market franchise that they might never be able to develop if they were to set up their own shop.

In recent years, S&Ls in Florida have been an attractive

target for interlopers, because they have historically done better than commercial banks in the state and because of the large amount of retirees with pension money. In 1983, BankAmerica Corporation, the holding company for Bank of America, bought the troubled Seafirst Bank in Washington State. Citicorp has recently expanded its nationwide coverage by buying up an S&L in California.

Eventually, interstate banking is expected to be fully legalized, and the major players are preparing for this eventuality by lining up as many customers across the country as they can. When interstate banking does become a reality, and the large money center banks begin operations across the country, many of the regional banks will have to work very hard to protect their positions. The larger banks will be trying to steal away customers and will be extremely aggressive in doing so. To protect against this, Massachusetts, Connecticut, and Rhode Island recently passed legislation that allows banks in these three states to merge with each other—across state lines. Many other states appear to be following suit. Such mergers will allow smaller institutions to combine forces and fight off the money center banks. In addition, some of the major regionals have started acquiring other banks, to make it more difficult for their money center competitors. NCNB Corporation (the holding company of North Carolina National Bank) and Mellon Bank are two examples.

ORGANIZATION—INSIDE THE BANK

Each bank has a unique internal organization. The chart on page 47 suggests how a big bank might be structured and how the responsibilities might be divided among various divisions. We strongly suggest that, before going to an interview, you get a copy of the annual report and make sure you have a good understanding of how that particular bank is organized.

Retail Banking Division

The retail division of a bank provides services to individual consumers and small- to middle-market companies through a

THE MONEY JOBS COMMERCIAL BANK

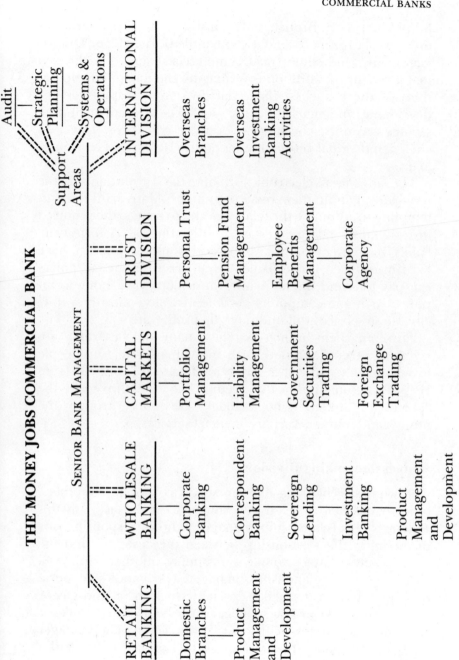

SENIOR BANK MANAGEMENT

Support Areas
- Audit
- Strategic Planning
- Systems & Operations

RETAIL BANKING
- Domestic Branches
- Product Management and Development

WHOLESALE BANKING
- Corporate Banking
- Correspondent Banking
- Sovereign Lending
- Investment Banking
- Product Management and Development

CAPITAL MARKETS
- Portfolio Management
- Liability Management
- Government Securities Trading
- Foreign Exchange Trading

TRUST DIVISION
- Personal Trust
- Pension Fund Management
- Employee Benefits Management
- Corporate Agency

INTERNATIONAL DIVISION
- Overseas Branches
- Overseas Investment Banking Activities

47

branch network. Branch staff consists of tellers, operations officers, platform officers* (who handle personal loans, mortgage loans, and some small commercial loans), and branch management. In addition to managing the day-to-day operations of the branches, the retail division is responsible for developing and marketing the products offered, including savings accounts, checking accounts, credit cards, traveler's checks, individual retirement accounts (IRAs), and consumer loans.

The advent of electronic banking has revolutionized the way banks handle their retail operations. Many banks are attempting to automate the teller line and to reduce the required investment in staff, real estate, and heating oil. A few of the banks, including Chemical Bank and Bank of America, have even introduced home banking systems, whereby customers can pay bills and initiate bank transactions via a home computer. As home computers become a reality, and not a novelty, these services will undoubtedly proliferate.

Through their branch systems, many of the banks are trying to target high-net-worth individuals—wealthy people to whom they can sell a variety of financial products, from IRAs to automatic lines of credit. They have invented the "personal banker," who manages accounts through the branch and markets various financial services.

Wholesale Banking Division

The wholesale banking division serves corporate customers, other banks, and foreign governments. At the heart of this system is the relationship manager, who is responsible for maintaining the relationship between the customer and the bank, whether the customer is a country, another bank, or a corporation. A relationship manager who handles corporations may have a particular specialty, such as oil and gas or high technology; or the manager may be assigned to cover companies within a specific geographic region. The manager really has two jobs—that of a marketing officer and that of a credit analyst. As a marketing officer, the manager sells the appropriate products and services offered by the bank to the corporation. The officer may be assisted in this effort by specialty groups within the bank responsible for a product or group of products.

As a credit analyst, the officer evaluates a firm's financial condition and its ability to repay loans. The decision of whether or not to extend credit is usually made in conjunction with the report of a credit administrator, whose primary function is to review and then approve or reject credit decisions. Many banks have a credit committee system, whereby the officer presents recommendations for loan requests to a group of senior credit administrators.

CORBANKING

Banks manage their relationships with one another through their corbanking* (correspondent banking) departments. Every day billions of dollars are transferred among banks, and the corbanking group is responsible for handling this flow of funds. Usually the corbanking account officer oversees banks within a specific domestic or international region. There is often a separate section within corbanking for product development and implementation.

Maintaining good relations with other banks is essential for additional business. For instance, if one bank has a loan customer who wants more money than the bank can offer, it can sell out portions of the loan to its correspondent banks.

INVESTMENT BANKING

Recently, the wholesale divisions of commercial banks have instituted investment banking groups. They provide the bank's corporate customers with a basket of investment banking products, such as private placements, loan syndications, and merger and acquisition advisory services. Commercial banks must tread very carefully in this area in order not to violate the Glass-Steagall Act, which was enacted to prevent commercial banks and investment banks from getting into each other's business. As we have seen, however, Glass-Steagall left room for interpretation, and commercial banks have been permitted to offer some products without violating the letter of the law. Investment banking groups in commercial banks are usually structured along the same lines as corporate

49

finance departments in investment banking firms—except, of course, that they do not underwrite equity issues.

International Division

A bank's operations overseas are usually handled out of an international division. This area is responsible for delivering the bank's services worldwide, either to U.S. corporations with operations abroad or to foreign-owned entities. For instance, if General Electric wanted to construct a factory in Taiwan, it might use a U.S. bank with operations in Taiwan for financial support. GE might have a need for Taiwan dollar financing, or it might want to open a bank account so that it could manage its payroll. All the major U.S. banks have branches in the capital cities of Europe, Latin America, Asia, and Africa that provide services primarily to corporations abroad. Like the domestic division of the bank, the international division is staffed with branch management and support staff, as well as with lending officers and credit officers responsible for managing the overseas loan portfolio.

Capital Markets Division

In general, lending officers and credit departments manage the assets of the banks—that is, its loan portfolio. But banks have bonds and other assets that are handled by the bank's own investment managers, who generally work in the capital markets* group. The goal of this operation is to maximize the return the bank is making on its securities portfolio, while ensuring that the money is not tied up for too long, or too short, a time.

Determining the bank's funding strategy—sometimes called liability management—is usually the responsibility of a group within the capital markets division. In order to make loans, a bank first has to fund itself (find the money to lend out). Traditionally, this money came mostly from consumer savings and checking accounts. But because banks can no longer rely on savings and checking accounts, the task of liability management has become increasingly sophisticated and, in an era of volatile interest rates, highly risky.

In the 1970s banks found themselves with a "mismatch" problem—they were giving out 15- to 20-year mortgages at 6 percent and then having to fund themselves (purchase liabilities) at 15 percent. As a result many have become wary about committing an interest rate for a long period of time. For this reason, if a corporate customer asks an account officer for a 10-year $20 million loan to construct a widget factory at a fixed rate of interest, the account officer may have to make a special request for a liability manager to obtain this money for the customer and lock in a rate. In general, commercial banks prefer to make floating rate loans. If a company needs fixed-rate, long-term money, they can access the bond or private placement market.

The capital markets division also handles government securities, trading for the bank and for outside investors in the same way an investment bank would. The major money center banks and some of the larger regional and California banks are active in foreign exchange trading—that is, exchanging the currency of one nation for the currency of another nation. The traders in the "FX*room" trade both for the bank's clients and on behalf of the bank itself. When trading for a client's account, the trader makes a spread or commission whether the client makes or loses money. However, with trades made for the bank, if currencies don't move in the direction the trader has anticipated, the bank stands to lose money.

Trust Division

The trust division of a bank is entrusted with funds or duties for the benefit of others. Trust officers are often commissioned to oversee employee benefits plans or to invest the proceeds of pension funds for their client companies. They also service high-net-worth customers, people with large sums of money to invest, by helping them manage their finances and personal investments.

Trust officers also perform the duties of corporate agents.

For example, if a company issues a bond, the bank may act as trustee and, as such, be responsible for protecting the interests of the bondholders. Corporate agents may also handle the operational aspects of securities issues, by printing certificates, distributing dividends, and managing other parts of shareholder relations.

Only the trust division of a commercial bank is permitted to trade in the stock market on behalf of clients. For this reason, there are usually a number of stock analysts on staff, much as in a brokerage firm or investment bank. The corporate lending side of a bank is not supposed to communicate with the trust department because if the trust analysts were to learn that a particular company was having trouble making its loan payments, they could be accused of trading on insider information. The division between commercial lending and trust is often referred to in the industry as the "Chinese Wall."

Support Areas

In addition to the five main functional areas of the bank discussed above, there are a number of support activities, including strategic planning, auditing, and operations. Strategic planners analyze market trends and help senior management determine what direction the bank should take. Auditors manage the accounting systems in the bank and investigate trouble spots. Operations personnel are concerned with the flow of work throughout the organization and may be involved in systems development—finding efficient ways of channeling information and work. Their duties often include working with computers.

JOB OPPORTUNITIES

The diversity of operations within a bank requires a variety of employees with expertise in different areas. Commercial banks, therefore, often run several different training programs, each with a different orientation. The majority of entry-level opportunities are in retail banking (branch banking), corporate lending, product specialty areas, or operations, the division that provides "back office" support for the rest of the bank. The larger banks may also offer jobs in the investment banking and trading areas.

Retail Banking

For many years, retail bankers working on the floor of a branch (the area where customers are serviced) were stigmatized as the "poor relations" of the corporate lenders working upstairs, who were far away from the tedium of the tellers' lines. The work was considered operational and did not appear to require a great deal of imagination. Entry-level positions in retail banking, however, should not be written off. A position as a personal banker, for instance, will give an ambitious college or business school graduate sales experience and the opportunity to see concrete, measurable results early on. One recruiter considers sales experience extremely important for young people to acquire, particularly BAs who might be considering going to business school later.

Retail management training programs are designed to prepare young people to take on managerial positions within the branch, with authority to make loans to individuals and perhaps small businesses. Because corporate-level training programs are designed to produce only bank–customer relationship managers, BAs or MBAs interested in supervisory jobs, which provide an opportunity to be responsible for the professional development of a number of people early on, might consider retail bank training programs.

Corporate Lending

The increasing competition for corporate business has expanded the job of the corporate bank account officer to include going out into the marketplace and actively soliciting corporate business. Today, account officers have to be fairly sophisticated businesspeople who can walk into a treasurer's office at a client organization and discuss a wide range of topics. During a customer call,* a bank representative may have to answer questions on anything from interest rate forecasts to the bank's policy on unfriendly acquisitions. The ideal account officer is able to absorb limitless amounts of information and then present it to clients in an articulate and concise fashion. Of course, no one can know everything, but account officers are expected to have a thorough understanding of the bank, its policies, current events, and the operations of the client in question. As far as the customer is concerned, the calling officer *is* the bank. The bank, in turn, knows this and places a great deal of responsibility on the account officer.

Selling skills are extremely important to the success of a lending officer. Very often, knowing which of the bank's products best suit the customer's needs, and selling them successfully, is the skill that determines whether or not the bank makes money. A calling officer will eventually be evaluated on the basis of how much business he or she brings home.

Every year, an organization called Greenwich Research Associates (GRA) questions various corporations and compiles reports on how account officers at different banks are perceived in the marketplace. GRA was the brainstorm of a couple of bankers formerly with Morgan Guaranty who recognized how important account officers were to the overall success of a bank. The major banks are very sensitive to their GRA evaluation and often use it as the basis for identifying potential areas in which their account officers need to improve.

Credit analysis skills are also very important in corporate lending. The loan officer must be able to understand new financing and accounting techniques and be able to spot when a company is headed for trouble. In many banks, account officers are ultimately responsible for credit decisions—and when a loan goes bad, the officer is held accountable.

Credit analysis and marketing skills are stressed in most account officer training programs. The formal training period usually lasts nine to eighteen months. Most banks require a substantial amount of classroom training. Because of the increasing complexities of the business, however, training has become an ongoing process, even for officers who have been at the institution for many years.

In the investment banking area, training is usually modeled on the "associate pool" method used in investment banking firms. Trainees are placed in a group, or pool,* and are rotated for a period of time among the different functional areas of the bank's investment banking group. Assignments during this time usually depend on where the greatest need is within the corporate lending division. After their rotational period, trainees are assigned to a specific area. Usually, an MBA is required to join the division as a permanent employee, but commercial banks are less strict in this regard than investment banks. As with investment banking, training for a trading position in a commercial bank is mostly on the job. The trainee may spend a period of months simply observing what the seasoned traders do. Traders are hired at both the BA and MBA levels.

Product Specialist Areas

Many banks also run training programs for product specialists. New hires at the entry level are coached on a particular product or group of products to be marketed to corporate customers. Product specialist trainees may assist the account officer in targeting customers who are interested in a particular bank service. They may also take part in the marketing, follow-up, and support of the product after it is sold. Areas for specialization include international services, cash management, and leasing. Although the product specialist programs do not provide as broad a training experience as account officer training programs, they are well suited to individuals who have already decided on the aspect of commercial banking they want to focus on. These positions may be particularly attractive to MBAs who do not want to be in the classroom environment typical of the account officer programs. In addition, it is not uncommon to move from a product specialist position into an account officer slot, or vice versa, after a few years of experience.

Ameritrust
900 Euclid Avenue
Cleveland, Ohio 44101
(216) 687-5000

Ameritrust is a Cleveland-based bank with approximately 80 branches around the city and 120 branches statewide. It is part of the fifty-eighth largest bank holding company* in the United States and considers itself a strong player in the commercial lending market. Recently, Ameritrust has started up specialized lending groups in energy and in special industries (including health care, communications, and electronics).

Ameritrust has two training programs: one for retail banking and one for corporate lending. The retail program lasts a year and begins at the branch level, where trainees learn how to be tellers and how to handle branch operations. Trainees then move to the credit department where they spend an average of one or two months number-crunching and performing credit analyses of corporations. Subsequently, they return to the branch, where they handle loan applications, assume a supervisory role, and perhaps work on special projects with the branch manager. Between five and ten candidates are chosen for this program every year, most of them BAs. Of this group, 75 percent end up as branch managers, and 25 percent go into product areas, such as IRAs and discount brokerage, or into other services handled through the branch network.

The corporate banking training program is specifically designed to turn out loan officers. The program lasts around a year for MBAs and fifteen months for BAs. BAs who apply should have some accounting courses. Each year the bank hires four to five MBAs and eight to ten BAs for the program. The first four weeks of class training include the Omega course (see the Pittsburgh National Bank listing for a further description), a uniform credit analysis course, and a review of the American Bankers Association's handbooks on "statement spreading," or how to number-crunch. The class is taught by internal staff. Trainees also participate in a "skills for success" seminar that relies on role playing and videotape for teaching selling skills. During this period, speakers are brought in from the various parts of the bank to discuss their operations.

Trainees then move to the credit department, where they perform credit analyses in support of the line officers. This experience gives them the opportunity to interact with account officers and, conversely, gives the officers a chance to check out the new blood. After spending a number of months in credit, trainees begin interviewing for a permanent position. They then spend six months in an internship, with the understanding that if everything works out, they will become permanent employees of their chosen division.

BAs in the corporate banking training program make $17,000 to $18,000 to start, with MBAs making $22,000 to $30,000, depending on school and prior work experience. Salaries for retail banking trainees are somewhat lower. Benefits include medical plan, life insurance, tuition reimbursement (100 percent for career- or degree-oriented courses with a C or better, available after three months of employment), free checking, preferential loan rates, and an employee savings and investment plan (after one year employees put 2 percent to 15 percent of their base salary into the fund and the bank matches it dollar for dollar up to 6 percent).

Bank of America
P.O. Box 37000
San Francisco, California
94137
(415) 622-3456

335 Madison Avenue
New York, New York 10017
(212) 503-7000

555 South Flower Street
Los Angeles, California
90071
(213) 228-4567

233 South Wacker Drive
Chicago, Illinois 60606
(312) 876-1400

BofA, as it is affectionately known, is part of the second largest bank holding company in the United States. (It had been the largest, but at the present time Citibank holds that distinction.) In the good old days of "3-6-3" banking (see page 41), BofA set up a vast branch network in California, invading cities until it seemed as though there was a branch on every block! This proved to be an expensive proposition, and in the last few years the bank has been cutting back on its branch network. At the same time, BofA has been diversifying its operations. In 1983 it swallowed up the troubled Seafirst Bank in Washington State, as well as Charles Schwab, a highly successful nationwide discount brokerage firm. BofA has also been making a concerted effort to establish itself in the Northeastern marketplace, and its New York operation competes head-on with the likes of Bankers Trust, Morgan Guaranty, Citibank, and Chase.

The bank runs two major training programs—one for the California corporate banking division and one for the North America division. The California division operates over 40 corporate banking offices out of branches located throughout the state. Its primary line of business is middle-market lending. Account officers in the North America division handle the larger, Fortune 500* corporate accounts.

Each year, the bank hires approximately 90 BAs and MBAs, 70 percent of whom are slated for account officer positions in the California corporate banking division, with the remainder going into the North America division. When new hires come into the bank, they are assigned a sponsor—a senior account officer charged with responsibility for the trainees' development. Training lasts for about a year and is a combination of on-the-job and classroom instruction. Classes are taught at a training facility in Los Angeles, and courses are given in financial markets, credit analysis, accounting, bank management, banking and corporate law, operations, and international finance. Seminars are also given on the bank's products and services. Instruction is given by BofA staffers and outside professors. The emphasis is on case study, and teamwork is encouraged.

On-the-job work for the California corporate bankers consists of rotations through a number of areas in the bank, including operations, real estate, retail banking, and commercial lending. In addition, trainees complete "learner-controlled instruction," a self-paced course of study that operates under the supervision of the trainees' sponsors. In the North America division, on-the-job work consists of providing backup support for sponsors. Trainees write credit analyses, clear up operational problems, and in some cases go on customer calls.

In general, BAs start at $21,000-plus, and MBAs start at $30,000 and up. New York levels are usually somewhat higher than California. Benefits include major medical and dental coverage, life insurance, reduced loan rates, free checking, savings incentive (after three years), reduced Visa card rates, reduced commissions on stock transactions, and reduced mortgage rates.

Bank of Boston
100 Federal Street
Boston, Massachusetts 02110
(617) 434-2200

Here's an interesting fact about Bank of Boston (BOB): It has the largest physical presence of any U.S. bank in Argentina, with numerous branches throughout Latin America. BOB is part of the twentieth largest bank holding company in the United States, and is the largest bank in New England. It has also just celebrated its two-hundredth anniversary.

The bank runs a loan officer development program for five divisions—commercial, international, Massachusetts, multinational, and specialized corporate financing. The program lasts from 12 to 21 months. Training is broken down into separate phases, usually four for BAs and three for MBAs.

BAs with no prior work experience who join the bank take on a four-month on-the-job assignment designed to give them the chance to learn what banking is all about before starting classes. They then join the MBAs for Phase I of the official program, which is administered by the credit department. Classes in basic and intermediate accounting, credit analysis, corporate finance, international finance, and money and banking are taught by both in-house staff and outside professors. Case studies, presentations, and papers are required, and about two hours' worth of homework is assigned daily.

Phase II consists of two to three rotations through different divisions of the bank, with each stay lasting around three months. BAs who have done their preclass "internships" go through one less rotation than the others. In Phase III, trainees serve as backup to a loan officer for four to nine months, doing a great deal of number-crunching, after which they become loan officers themselves. Trainees going into the international division should be prepared to accept an overseas assignment when they reach loan officer level.

59

Each year 25 to 35 BAs are hired, and slightly more MBAs. Salaries begin at around $18,000 for BAs and $25,000-plus for MBAs. Benefits include major medical coverage, life insurance, and tuition reimbursement.

Bank of New England
28 State Street
Boston, Massachusetts 02106
(617) 742-4000

The Bank of New England is the fifty-seventh largest bank in the United States and serves primarily middle-market corporate customers in New England. The bank offers a structured training program for those interested in either lending or credit. A separate program is offered in the branch banking area.

A total of approximately 22 BAs, BSs, MBAs, or individuals with significant work experience are considered for the lending and credit training program. Although not required, formal training in accounting and finance is helpful, particularly for candidates considering a career in credit administration.

Training for credit and lending is broken down into two phases. Both the lending and credit people go through Phase I, which begins with one to two months of orientation followed by rigorous on-the-job training. Trainees are assigned to the credit department, where they analyze financial statements and industry statistics and trends. Their work is supplied to the lending officers, and sometimes trainees go out on calls with an established officer. BAs stay in the credit department anywhere from two to three years, while MBAs move on after about one year.

For those going into lending, Phase II consists of an assignment to a lending group. The trainee gradually progresses from serving as administrative backup to having solo calling responsibilities. Phase II for credit trainees consists of an assignment as credit section manager, with direct responsibility for five to seven trainees; as special industries senior analyst, to develop expertise in the credit criteria for specific industries; or as loan review officer. These assignments are designed to develop the trainee's analytical and administrative skills.

During Phase I and Phase II of the program, both groups participate in the Loan Officer Training System (LOTS), which consists of eleven seminars held every three weeks. These seminars are taught by line officers and cover such topics as cash management, bankruptcy, money market instruments, international services, prospecting,* fee-based and credit services, problem loans, asset-based financing,* and specialized lending. "Mastery tests" are administered at the conclusion of each unit. Trainees are expected to participate in group discussions and are evaluated on the basis of test results and classroom participation.

The Bank of New England also offers a two-year retail banking training program, divided into four phases, that is designed to prepare new hires for positions as branch administrators and branch lending officers. Approximately eighteen candidates are hired per year. In Phase I, trainees are introduced to deposits and loans by serving as tellers and operations staff members. They also learn about retail loan applications, credit decisions, credit investigations, loan documentation, and loan collection. During Phase II, trainees are assigned to a specific branch for instruction in marketing techniques and coaching in the products and services offered to retail customers. In Phase III, trainees become supervisors, in charge of the tellers and customer services representatives. At this stage, trainees report directly to the branch manager. As new supervisors, trainees will be included in a number of seminars designed to enhance their managerial skills. Phase IV consists of a twelve-week course in making loans, supplemented by on-the-job experience in the assigned branch.

The bank also offers a less structured program in the operations department. The program lasts for approximately three months and consists of rotations through a number of units, including adjustments, cash management and customer payroll sales, check processing, fraud control, and funds transfer. Trainees are promoted to supervisors after one to two years of employment.

Salaries for BAs begin at $19,000 and MBAs start in the

high twenties to mid-thirties. Benefits include medical insurance, IRAs, pension plan, tuition reimbursement, company thrift plan (after one year the bank will match 50 percent of an employee's contribution, which can range from 2 percent to 12 percent of base salary), free checking, and a subsidized mass transit pass.

Bankers Trust
280 Park Avenue
New York, New York 10017
(212) 775-2500

At Bankers Trust, part of the tenth largest bank holding company in the United States, trainees are taught to achieve "excellence through common purpose," a slogan that has become central to BT's corporate culture. Well, something must be working, because Bankers Trust's account officers are considered among the best in the business—right up there with the perennial favorite, Morgan Guaranty. BT also happens to be one of the best-performing banks in the United States.

Each year Bankers Trust hires about 90 BAs and MBAs to pursue the account officer training program, which appears to be quite rigorous. Some trainees report spending "every waking hour" on homework assignments. After six weeks of on-the-job exposure, BAs take courses in money and banking, basic accounting, and corporate finance before joining the MBAs for courses in credit, advanced accounting, and international finance. Classes are taught by bank officers, as well as by Harvard Business School professors and by Robert Johnson of New York University.

As part of the "excellence through common purpose" objective, trainees are strongly encouraged to help each other through the program. One MBA trainee was reprimanded by her supervisor for not helping out weaker students. At BT, financial incentives are given to team players. Trainees characterize the atmosphere as competitive but cooperative.

Trainees are evaluated by the training director, who is an account officer of the bank on rotation, and by the head of the training center, who is a professional trainer. Exams and individual presentations and projects are weighted most heavily. On-the-job performance, teamsmanship, sales ability, and interpersonal skills are also considered. Some trainees are forced to drop out of the program, but those who stay are promoted to assistant treasurer after approximately one year.

BT also runs a program for its investment banking operation. Of all the commercial banks, BT is considered to have made the greatest inroads in competing head-on with the biggest names on Wall Street. Each year the bank hires about five MBAs with previous work experience. All training is on the job. Trainees are placed in an associate pool so they can gain experience in a number of different areas within the bank. During this time, they assist officers in making transactions from both the analytical and marketing points of view.

BT also has a money market training program for those interested in trading operations. The bank looks for majors in economics or finance and hires ten to fifteen people a year. Trainees go through two to three months of classroom work and spend the rest of the training period on the floor, observing the seasoned traders.

There is also a formal twelve-month program in banking operations. About fifteen people a year are hired to undergo a combination of classroom and on-the-job training. Instruction is given in management systems and data processing. After one year, trainees become supervisors and oversee anywhere from fifteen to twenty-five employees. New supervisors are responsible for employee management as well as for the project to which they are assigned.

BT also hires a handful of MBAs to go into strategic planning. This division assists senior management in planning the future direction of the bank. A position in strategic planning usually lasts only about three years, after which time the employee is rotated to another division of the bank.

BAs usually start at $24,000, sometimes higher, especially in the trading area, where BAs start in the upper twenties and can earn a bonus. MBAs start at around $34,000, which can rise up to the low forties in some divisions. Benefits include medical coverage, life insurance, free checking, savings plan (up to 6 percent of salary is matched by the bank), and tuition reimbursement. In addition, the bank offers supplemental compensation to top performers through a bonus program.

Centerre BanCorporation
One Centerre Plaza
St. Louis, Missouri 63101
(314) 554-6000

Centerre is part of the sixty-eighth largest bank holding company in the United States. A regional bank operating in twelve states in the Midwest, the bank recently made a strategic decision to focus on middle-market companies for future business development.

Centerre's account officer development program lasts one year and is designed to provide new commercial banking employees with the background needed to begin their career. The bank hired one MBA and nine BAs during the 1984 recruiting season. Trainees begin the program as commercial banking analysts in the training division and then are assigned to one of several commercial lending divisions.

The first half of the training year is spent participating in a wide variety of seminars on bank management, bank operations, and commercial lending. During this time, new analysts take on working assignment in these areas. The objective is to give new hires a base of knowledge so that they will be able to work within the bank's established policies and procedures. The second half of the year is spent reviewing and analyzing existing and proposed loan situations at Centerre Bank. Analysts work closely with account officers from all the commercial lending divisions on live loan situations, developing a broad-based understanding of commercial lending and commercial account management.

After completing this first year, analysts become commercial banking representatives and are assigned to one of the commercial banking divisions. At the same time, they take seminars in marketing, corporate services, and other commercial banking topics.

Salaries start at $19,500 for BAs and in the mid-twenties for MBAs. Benefits include major medical and dental coverage, life insurance, free checking, reduced credit card rates, reduced mortgage and personal loan rates, tuition reimbursement, a savings incentive plan, and subsidized bus fares.

Central National Bank
800 Superior Avenue
Cleveland, Ohio 44114
(216) 344-3000

Central National Bank offers two main training programs: one for corporate lending and one for retail banking. Usually only MBAs are hired for corporate lending, while BAs go into the retail side. Approximately twelve trainees are hired each year, some internally. BAs are expected to have some knowledge of accounting before joining the bank.

Trainees in the corporate lending program and the retail program attend separate classes in credit analysis. An internal credit manager leads the classes, which consist of case studies and two-minute credit drills. Teamwork is encouraged. The retail program also includes structured training in such areas as operations, credit, and sales and business development.

Corporate banking trainees also attend seminars in business development. For example, a trainee may be involved in a two-month project with a vice president of the corporation that involves preparing market analyses, identifying prospects, and going on cold calls.*

During the training period, which lasts about eighteen months for retail trainees and eighteen months to two years for corporate trainees, the training director serves as supervisor. Trainees are also formally evaluated about once a month on a scale of 1 to 5 by the leaders of the specific classes or seminars. They also evaluate their own performance. About 10 percent of the trainees do not make it through the program. Because CNB recruits trainees from within the bank, it is also possible to get into the program indirectly by joining the bank in a support staff position.

Salaries begin at $16,000-plus for BAs and $23,000-plus for MBAs depending on prior work experience. Benefits include 100 percent tuition reimbursement for business-related courses or degrees, major medical coverage, life insurance, and free checking accounts.

Chase Manhattan Bank
One Chase Manhattan Plaza
New York, New York 10081
(212) 552-2222

Part of the third largest bank holding company in the United States, Chase has had some image problems in recent years. Like Continental Illinois and Seafirst, the bank was involved in the Penn Square Bank fiasco (see the Continental listing for a fuller discussion). If this wasn't enough, the bank also had to contend with paying the bills for Drysdale, a New York securities firm that went under and left Chase responsible for its obligations. These two problems left Chase with over $200 million in loan losses. The bank has come a long way in healing itself, but the effort has slowed down Chase's progress on other fronts. For instance, the bank is considered less aggressive than competitors like Citibank and Bank of America in its efforts to diversify into other areas of the financial services industry.

Chase takes a centralized approach to training its relationship managers. Throughout the year, trainees hired from all over the United States join classes of about 30 people, some with only BAs and others with various graduate degrees, including MBAs and masters in international affairs, for the bank's one-year credit development program. Chase hires a large number of people each year, depending on the bank's needs and the economy. In 1984, for example, they hired approximately 170 people for the credit development program. Chase's philosophy toward training has altered somewhat recently, with an eye toward making it more responsive to the financial services marketplace. The credit program continues to be strong in teaching technical skills, but emphasis is now being placed equally on developing marketing and selling skills.

Training begins with one week of orientation. Inside staff as well as outside instructors speak on the nature of the organization, its customer base, and the marketplace in which it

66

operates. Trainees then move into one to three months of classroom instruction. Courses include corporate finance, accounting, the regulatory environment, technology, international finance, marketing and selling, risk assessment, and financial statement analysis. After classes are completed, trainees spend approximately three months on the job. During this time they learn the operations of a given business unit—the nuts and bolts of how things get done and how customers interact with the bank. Trainees then go through a six-month stint in credit analysis training. They work on real cases and learn how to make complete analyses of bank customers. Participants are asked to prepare cases independently for presentation to bank officers. Trainees report that the casework is an important part of the overall evaluation process. Chase's program has a reputation for being very tough and has an attrition rate of around 10 percent.

Salaries for BAs begin in the low to mid-twenties; MBAs start in the low thirties to mid-forties. Benefits include Blue Cross/Blue Shield, discount travel packages, discount theater tickets, profit sharing, employee store, free checking, and tuition reimbursement.

Chemical Bank
277 Park Avenue
New York, New York 10172
(212) 310-6161

Chemical is part of the sixth largest bank holding company in the United States and serves retail customers through about 270 branches in the New York metropolitan area as well as corporate customers worldwide. The bank's major strengths are its strong retail operation and its established middle-market customer base.

Chemical runs a training program for lending officers. Both MBAs and BAs are accepted each year, and they are expected to choose from one of four divisions for final placement up front: metropolitan (middle-market lending), world banking–domestic, world banking–international, and world banking–real estate.

For BAs, classwork comprises four months of the program,

which lasts about seven months. Classes go for seven hours each day and instruction is given in basic and advanced accounting, business analysis, economics, money and banking, and corporate finance. Classes are usually given two at a time —one in the morning and the other in the afternoon. Outside professors are brought in. Trainees receive grades for each course and take a final exam at the conclusion of each segment. Analytical exercises are expected to be done daily and are submitted at the end of each week. Trainees must pass the basic accounting exam to continue in the program.

MBAs undergo accelerated classroom instruction. They are not required to take the economics course or the money and banking course. The most demanding portion of the training is a ten-week session of case studies. Trainees are given one case per week and are expected to complete it on their own in three or four days. Solutions are then reviewed by Chemical line officers.

After the class and case study segments, trainees go through three one-month rotations. International trainees are assigned directly to their unit, as are MBAs who were directly hired into the division. Those who do rotate go through assignments in various lending sections. At the end of the rotation period individuals are placed in a division where their interests and the bank's requirements best match. Trainees report that the competition is extremely stiff. BAs receive officers' titles approximately eighteen months after they start with the bank; the period is shorter for MBAs.

Salaries for BAs start at $22,000 to $23,000, with MBAs starting in the low to mid-thirties. Benefits include Major Medical and dental coverage, life insurance, free checking, reduced loan and credit card rates, a savings incentive plan, reduced stock commissions, and tuition reimbursement. Chemical Bank's world headquarters has an excellent employee cafeteria subsidized by the company.

Citibank
399 Park Avenue
New York, New York 10043
(212) 559-1000

Citibank's hiring process is more decentralized than that of most other banks, so it might be wise to contact the division at which you seek employment rather than the centralized recruiting office. One word of warning: Do not be fooled by Citi's glossy recruiting brochure featuring the Citicorp building, a recent dramatic addition to Manhattan's skyline. Not all Citibank employees actually work there. Most work in 399 Park a block away, where the rent isn't so high!

Citibank is the major component of the largest bank holding company in the United States and is a mammoth operation. Shy, retiring personality types are not encouraged to join. One former trainee put it this way: "Citibank is not a hand-holding organization." Candidates should be tough, have a secure sense of themselves, and be able to handle criticism.

Citi has a training program for corporate lenders that accepts upwards of 40 BAs, MAs (usually in international relations), and MBAs each year. The amount varies, depending on the demands of the marketplace and the economy. New hires begin training in the area to which they will later be permanently assigned. They spend two to three months getting used to the office and serving in a backup capacity. They learn the bank's credit policies and internal procedures. Following this, trainees attend classes—the coursework is more extensive for BAs than for MBAs. Instruction is given in accounting, corporate finance, analytical accounting, and credit analysis. There is a midterm and a final in each course. Classes are taught by bank staff as well as by professors from Fordham, New York University, Harvard, and the University of Virginia. Trainees then go into a project phase in which they perform analyses on live credit decisions. A given project can last from three weeks to six months. Program supervisors try to assign trainees projects that will build their weaker skills.

Citibank is definitely an innovative bank and an exciting

69

place to work. Just be prepared. Trainees report spending four to six hours each night on homework, more on weekends. The atmosphere is filled with pressure, and trainees who don't make the mark may very well be asked to leave.

Salaries start in the middle to upper twenties for BAs and in the high twenties to low thirties for MBAs. Benefits include major medical and dental coverage, life insurance, reduced loan rates, discounts on credit cards, and tuition reimbursement.

Citizens and Southern National Bank
35 Broad Street
Atlanta, Georgia 30399
(404) 581-2121

C&S is one of the 50 largest regional banks in the United States. The bank offers two major structured training programs—one for commercial lending and one for community banking. Training in other areas, such as auditing, factoring, trust, and operations generally takes place on the job.

The community banking program takes approximately 25 to 30 BAs each year for training in branch management positions. The program lasts from twelve to fourteen months and combines classroom and on-the-job training. For instance, trainees may spend one week in a teller workshop, followed by two weeks working as a teller; or one week in a customer service workshop, followed by two weeks working as a customer service officer. After the program is completed, C&S decides, in conjunction with the trainee, on the best area for permanent placement. Trainees may go through a stint in auditing and personnel and then move into an assistant manager or manager position. Or, if trainees are judged to be fairly strong in accounting and finance, they can go to "credit school" and take up a lending position in a branch, structuring loans for small companies based in Atlanta.

C&S's commercial lending management program accepts approximately six to eight MBAs and sixteen to eighteen BAs per year for preparation as lending officers. Trainees spend three to six months working in a branch, getting used to banking in general and C&S in particular. Rotations take the trainees through teller training, customer service, and installment loans. Then, as in the community banking program, "credit school" begins. There are two straight months of classes—one month in accounting and one in finance. Papers are assigned and tests are given by professors brought in from Georgia State. Next, trainees spend six to eight months doing case studies on real credit situations in the bank and performing background credit work for the lending officers. After the program, trainees join the commerical banking group as permanent employees.

C&S also hires entry-level candidates into auditing (fifteen per year), international (five to six MBAs per year), asset-based lending (six per year), trust (two per year), and operations (eight per year). All training for these areas is on the job.

Salaries begin at $15,000 to $18,000 for BAs and $21,000 to $25,000 for MBAs. Benefits include medical and dental coverage, long-term disability and life insurance, profit sharing, and retirement plan. BAs who pursue their MBA at night are reimbursed in full if their grades are acceptable.

Connecticut Bank and Trust
One Constitution Plaza
Hartford, Connecticut 06115
(203) 244-5000

Connecticut Bank and Trust will soon be merging with Bank of New England, but both institutions will do their own hiring and training. CBT services small and medium-size corporate and individual customers through 150 offices in the state. CBT's commercial customers are typically "single plant" operations that rely on the bank for such services as equipment financing and construction and real estate loans.

Each year CBT runs a corporate and commercial lending development program for BAs and MBAs who are interested in lending to corporations in the state. The bank would not disclose statistics on the numbers hired because there is significant variation from year to year. The program lasts a year for MBAs and eighteen months for BAs and consists of classroom instruction with weekly lectures held in the corporate credit department. The bank also holds seminars on such topics as credit, accounting, finance, economics, and legal issues. Trainees can bypass the accounting course by taking an exemption exam. After the classroom sessions, trainees go through rotations of one day to six weeks in commerical credit, real estate, corporate financial planning, bank investment, international bank and corporate services, consumer credit, loan review, branch banking, business credit, and bank operations. Toward the end of training, new hires work as analysts and serve in backup capacity to line officers analyzing credit requests and going on customer calls.

CBT also offers a training program in its trust department. Candidates spend one year rotating through the following divisions: investments, operations, marketing, and accounts management. In addition, trainees are given reading assignments and special projects designed to increase their knowledge of the trust function. Areas covered include investment research, portfolio management, securities trading, trust, real estate, and estate planning.

There is also a personal banking program that trains new hires for positions in the bank's retail network. For five months trainees rotate through a branch, working in consumer credit and operations. Following this, they either are permanently assigned and begin working or go through further training in preparation for a higher-level managerial role. Only a few are selected for this second path.

Candidates for the bank's auditing program are expected to have an extensive background in accounting. Courses offered include auditing techniques and responsibilities, financial reporting, bank accounting and control, and bank regulations. The program lasts from nine to twelve months.

Starting salaries are in the mid-twenties for MBAs and $16,500 for BAs. Benefits include contributory employee medical and dental insurance, contributory supplemental life insurance, contributory supplemental dependent medical and dental insurance, tuition aid, and a thrift plan. The bank also has a home ownership program that offers favorable downpayment financing and mortgage rates 1 percent below market.

Continental Bank
231 South LaSalle Street
Chicago, Illinois 60693
(312) 828-2345

Continental, part of the eighth largest bank holding company in the United States, has been having some serious financial difficulties recently that have been well documented in the press. The bank's problems began a few years ago with Penn Square Bank in Oklahoma. Penn Square reportedly sold almost $1 billion worth of energy-related loans to Continental and then went belly up, leaving Continental with a bunch of problem loans. The Penn Square incident left Continental with low earnings and low morale. Recently, the federal government has entered the picture—by providing support for Continental—thus permitting the bank to continue its operations. A new management team has been brought in, although strong doubts remain about Continental's future.

Continental Bank's wholesale banking service program offers training for account officer positions. The last we heard was that approximately 100 BSs, BBAs, and MBAs are hired for this program each year. This number may be subject to dramatic change depending on Continental's financial stability. BAs coming into Continental participate in three six-month rotations within the bank. Concurrently, they will enroll in courses (including intermediate accounting and corporate finance) in an MBA program at one of the area schools. They must receive a grade of B or better in order to enter the second part of the program, a six-month analytic phase. During this time the trainees work on case studies from the Harvard Business School and from within the bank and attend a series of lectures given by bank personnel. No exams are given within the bank—trainees are judged solely on their technical aptitude and their performance on the line. The program lasts from 18 to 24 months, after which time trainees are promoted from banking associates to banking officers. At this time, the training director makes a decision about appropriate permanent placement.

MBAs who come into the program, spend a few weeks in orientation, followed by a ten-week stint in the operations area. Then they enter the analytic phase, similar to that for BAs. Subsequently, they learn how to write credit reports and perform other bank analyses before going into one three-month assignment. Afterward, they are permanently placed. No MBAs are hired directly into a division.

Most graduates of the wholesale banking program go into backup assignments in the lending area, although a handful of MBAs may go into the investment banking department or the correspondent banking division. Continental also hires foreign nationals who are getting their MBA in the United States to staff overseas offices. Candidates for the bank's European, Middle Eastern, African, and Latin American divisions may go directly overseas for a while and return to headquarters in Chicago for further training. Candidates for the Asian division start training at headquarters.

The bank's financial information services/auditing program is designed to train individuals with some systems or accounting background in the bank's financial and accounting reporting systems. About 100 trainees enter each year as applications programmers, staff accountants, staff auditors, or account analysts. Training consists of a combination of classroom and hands-on experience in accounting, auditing, and data processing. Trainees are evaluated by the instructors throughout the program.

The real estate program, which accepts about ten candidates each year, is designed to turn out real estate lending officers. Candidates are expected to have a strong background in finance and accounting. Topics covered in training include market analysis and segmentation, appraisals, and the administration of real estate loans. Trainees are given two temporary line responsibilities for which they must meet certain minimum competency requirements. The program is designed to allow for customer contact early on.

Training in the leasing and bond and treasury services is basically on the job. The bond department has recently begun a more structured training program that includes a series of rotations through the different product areas within the department.

Continental offers starting salaries from $21,000 to $23,000 for BAs and from $30,000 to $35,000 for MBAs. Benefits include major medical and dental coverage, business travel accident insurance, life insurance, profit sharing, pension plan, and tuition reimbursement.

Crocker Bank
One Montgomery Street—West Tower
San Francisco, California 94104
(415) 983-2000

Crocker is the fourteenth largest bank in the country, with over 350 branches. It is majority-owned by Midland Bank PLC, a British bank. Crocker hasn't posted its best performance recently but is making a concerted effort to reinstill the "entrepreneurial spirit" in its employees.

At Crocker, all entry-level professionals are hired directly into a particular area. For this reason, the bank prefers candidates with specific interests and backgrounds rather than general knowledge. The approximate number of trainees hired in 1984 by each division is as follows: middle-market lending, ten BAs and ten MBAs; corporate lending, five BAs and four MBAs; personal banking, ten MBAs; and international, three BAs and three MBAs. All new hires go through a three-day orientation period during which time they are addressed by senior management and informed of Crocker's current strategic direction.

All staff slated for lending go through a loan officer development program. Since Crocker stresses on-the-job training, only about five weeks are spent in class. The courses cover corporate finance and a limited amount of accounting, loan structuring, loan administration, asset-based lending, and credit analysis. New hires can go into one of a number of divisions, including middle-market lending, corporate banking, and international. On-the-job training continues for another four to six months for MBAs and about a year for BAs.

The bank also hires about ten MBAs per year to join its personal banker development program, which combines classroom and on-the-job training. New hires are trained to become business development representatives in the branches and to sell bank services to high-net-worth customers. MBAs interested in money market trading can enter a three-month rotation program through money market securities, municipal bonds, foreign exchange, and public finance. After the rotations, trainees are permanently placed into one of these areas.

The bank also hires MBAs as associates in the corporate finance department, where they are trained as generalists. Associates work in a pool and may be assigned to projects in different areas, including M&A, private placements,* leveraged buyouts,* and financial consulting to emerging growth companies. Previous work experience in sophisticated financing techniques is preferred. The investment banking group has an incentive compensation plan, with bonuses awarded on the basis of individual performance.

Salaries start in the high teens to low twenties for BAs and in the high twenties to low thirties for MBAs. Benefits include major medical coverage, life insurance, discounted banking services, and a savings incentive plan.

European American Bank
10 Hanover Square
New York, New York 10015
(212) 437-4300

EAB is part of the thirty-second largest bank holding company in the United States and services corporate and retail customers. It is owned by a consortium of six European banks.

The bank has a highly structured twelve-month training program for middle-market, international, and national (large corporate) lending. Trainees are hired specifically for one of these areas. The program is run twice a year, in January and June, and there are about ten trainees per group. According to the bank, most of the trainees are BAs because MBAs tend to shy away from a program as structured as this one.

Upon joining the bank, trainees are placed in a pool, where they are on call for bank officers who need them for number-crunching or work on special projects. Trainees are assigned work by the training director. At the same time, they take an accelerated accounting course for twelve to fourteen weeks, taught by an outside professor. The course covers basic accounting through advanced accounting and includes homework and a number of written assignments. After the accounting course, trainees take an eight-week credit analysis/corporate finance class that focuses on case studies. Trainees are evaluated on the basis of their class performance—and they are expected to do well.

After their coursework, trainees remain in the trainee pool and support line officers performing credit-related work. On-the-job training is supplemented by seminars on the bank's products and services. Trainees are then assigned to the division for which they were originally hired. They serve as "territorial assistants" and become line officers within two years.

The company did not disclose salary or benefits information.

Federal Reserve System
Board of Governors of the Federal Reserve System
20th and C Streets NW
Washington, D.C. 20551
(202) 452-3000

The Federal Reserve system has three basic functions: to devise and implement monetary policy, to safeguard the movement of money in our economy, and to maintain a sound and competitive banking system. District banks are located in Boston, New York City, Philadelphia, Cleveland, Richmond, Atlanta, Chicago, St. Louis, Minneapolis, Kansas City, Dallas, and San Francisco. Each district bank does its own hiring, so it is best to contact the location nearest you.

The Fed* offers entry-level opportunities for BAs interested in bank examination. Bank examiners investigate banks and bank holding companies to ensure that they are following banking law and properly reporting and recording all transactions, profits, and losses. The examiners visit banks in the same way that auditors do. Examinations can last from two weeks to two months, depending on the particular bank involved.

The Federal Reserve system hires BAs each year for the bank examiner position. Training is on the job for the first nine months. Trainees then attend courses taught by the Fed on how to conduct a bank examination, what the rationale is for performing certain types of examinations, and how to recognize "red flags"—potential trouble spots—during an examination. It takes between four and five years to become a full-fledged bank examiner.

Salaries for this position start at approximately $18,000 (New York). Benefits include major medical and dental coverage, life insurance, pension plan, and tuition reimbursement.

Fidelity Bank
Broad and Walnut Streets
Philadelphia, Pennsylvania 19109
(215) 985-6000

A regional operation, Fidelity is part of the sixty-third largest bank holding company in the United States. The bank principally serves the Pennsylvania, New Jersey, Delaware, and Maryland markets and deals mostly with small and medium-size companies.

Fidelity's professional banker development program, which accepts approximately twenty people per year, mostly BAs, is designed to give those who aspire to management positions a broad understanding of the banking business. Trainees spend approximately four months rotating among the various divisions: corporate banking, finance and planning, money markets, financial management, community banking, information management, human resources, and accounting and auditing. Classroom instruction, case studies, and presentations are used, and candidates are evaluated on the basis of tests, presentations, and class participation. The second phase of the program is a six to seven month on-the-job assignment. Permanent placement is determined through a combination of the trainee's desires and the bank's needs.

Salaries begin at $17,000. Benefits include major medical and dental coverage, life insurance, pension plan, stock purchase plan, matched savings plan, and 100 percent tuition reimbursement.

First Chicago Corporation
One First National Plaza
Chicago, Illinois 60670
(312) 732-8048

First Chicago is part of the eleventh largest bank holding company in the nation. In 1980 Barry F. Sullivan, formerly of Chase Manhattan, took over as chairman and instituted some major organizational changes. The bank's financial performance has shown marked improvement during Sullivan's tenure, and industry surveys now rank First Chicago's account officers among the best.

First Chicago has two formal training programs: the First Scholar Program and the Relationship Management Development Program (RMDP). The First Scholar Program, which has been in existence for seventeen years, trains about 25 high-potential liberal arts majors with little or no background in accounting or finance to become bankers. Approximately one-third to one-half of all First Scholars are career changers. Participation in the program requires concurrent enrollment in the MBA program at either the University of Chicago or Northwestern. For this reason, recruiters like to see GMAT scores above 600. Those admitted work at the bank full time and take two courses per term at night. In-bank assignments consist of rotations through the commercial lending area, financial products (investment banking) operations, product marketing, and asset and liability management. After a number of rotations, tailored to individual needs, candidates are permanently placed. Trainees write learning objectives for each rotational assignment and are evaluated at the end. First Scholars do not necessarily end up as commercial lenders. A number find permanent spots in asset and liability management, for instance.

The Relationship Management Development Program is designed to turn out loan officers. Approximately 18 BAs and BBAs and 45 MBAs are chosen each year. During the summer, BAs sit through three months of intense classroom instruction in accounting, finance, and economics. Tests are administered almost weekly. In the fall BAs join the BBAs and MBAs for a thirteen-week program that introduces them to the bank and its products and services. The legal aspects of banking are also examined. Trainees then participate in a credit analysis workshop, during which time they study live cases sent over from the line. This phase lasts from two to six months, depending on how well the trainees perform industry analyses and circumstantial credit decisions. After this, they are permanently assigned. Trainees are evaluated every six months.

First Chicago offers starting salaries of $21,000 to $24,000 for BAs and $30,000 to $35,000 for MBAs. Benefits include major medical coverage, free lunch program, and tuition reimbursement (except during the classroom phase for RMDPs).

First City National Bank of Houston
1001 Main Street
Houston, Texas 77002
(713) 658-6011

First City is part of the twenty-third largest bank holding company in the United States and has offices throughout the state of Texas. As is true of many Texas banks, First City's earnings have been under some pressure recently because of the heavy concentration of energy loans in its portfolio.

First City has a highly structured three-phase professional bank training program that all entry-level professionals are required to go through. The bank hires approximately 25 BAs and 25 MBAs per year. Trainees can begin the program in either September or January. In Phase I, trainees come to Houston for a seven-week orientation course on bank management taught by in-house personnel. Representatives from various areas within the bank give trainees the lowdown on their jobs. After this, trainees attend a series of lectures given by university professors on accounting, corporate finance, cash flow analysis, and money and banking. Subsequently, new hires are introduced to the bank's products and services by product specialists and line officers.

After orientation, trainees attend five weeks of intensive credit training and four weeks of test review. "Credit school" consists of a combination of straight academics and credit skills development. Trainees are coached in reading and deciphering financial statements and are expected to prepare written analyses. Classes are given in advanced accounting and consolidating balance sheets of separate companies. Coursework is supplemented by a self-study program covering ratio analyses and pro formas* (projected financial statements). New hires are also introduced to loan officers and prepare loan reviews for them. In the last part of Phase I, line officers present case studies to trainees and introduce them to practical credit skills used in assessing the creditworthiness of customers and prospects.

The test review portion of Phase I is an intense four-week period during which trainees must independently analyze two credit applications and prepare written presentations. Finally, an oral presentation is made to a committee of loan and credit department officers. Because this period is so important in determining the future career path of trainees, it is taken quite seriously.

At the outset of Phase II, trainees choose whether to pursue a career in product delivery or relationship banking. This is usually a fairly clear-cut decision since it is based on the credit test period. For the product delivery people, phase II consists of rotations through the product areas, where they help formulate and implement business plans. Relationship managers attend advanced credit analysis courses and do case studies for companies in specialized industries. They also work directly with loan officers, helping them manage accounts and develop calling strategies.

Before Phase III, trainees are assigned to specific departments. Relationship managers typically end up in community banking, corporate banking, middle-market lending, small

81

business/retail, or specialized lending. Product delivery people go to marketing, operational delivery, product development, staff supervision, or technical support. Phase III is essentially the first four to six months of on-the-job training and is supplemented by workshops to refine trainees' skills. Initial assignments last from one to two years.

Salaries for BAs begin in the low twenties and MBAs start in the mid- to upper twenties. Benefits include major medical and dental coverage, life insurance, free checking, preferred rate personal loans, and a savings plan after one year.

First Interstate Bank of California
707 Wilshire Boulevard
Los Angeles, California 90017
(213) 614-4111

First Interstate Bancorp, the holding company of First Interstate Bank, operates twenty-one different banks in eleven Western states and is the seventh largest bank holding company in the United States. First Interstate is the flagship bank, with over 300 branches and 13,000 employees in California.

First Interstate's training philosophy is that the best way to learn is by doing. In keeping with this, all training programs are essentially on the job. The bank runs two programs—one for branches and one for corporate lending. There are two paths open to those entering the branch program: operations or credit. Operations trainees eventually become managers, overseeing a staff of anywhere from 10 to 200 employees. Credit trainees eventually become consumer credit officers. New hires in both operations and credit begin with a four- to six-month assignment in different functional areas of the branch—for example, opening and servicing accounts, branch accounting, and customer assistance. At this time, they are also trained in management and communication skills. After this, operations and credit trainees part ways. Operations trainees receive the rest of their training on the job, supplemented by additional instruction in management skills. Prospective credit officers spend four months studying consumer lending. Courses are held in credit, loan processing, loan interviewing, and loan documentation. All courses are taught by bank personnel. Trainees in this program include new hires as well as people who have come up through the ranks.

The corporate banking development program is designed to turn out loan officers, and it is geared toward those with a strong background in corporate finance and accounting. It lasts approximately one year for MBAs and eighteen months for BAs. Trainees begin the program in a branch, learning the nuts and bolts of banking. After this, they spend about fifteen weeks in the classroom. Courses in credit analysis, intermediate accounting, financial statement analysis, and legal documentation are taught by internal staff. Perhaps the most difficult part of the program—which, by the way, reportedly requires four hours of advance preparation per night—are two "mock loan" projects. Trainees are required to do extremely detailed analyses of companies and present their findings to a credit committee for review. After the program is over, trainees take up positions in the world banking group.

The bank would not disclose salary information, although they did say First Interstate was competitive with other banks in its marketplace. Benefits include major medical and dental coverage, life insurance, reduced loan rates (after one year), and discounts on credit cards.

First National Bank of Atlanta
2 Peachtree Street NW
Atlanta, Georgia 30383
(404) 588-5000

First Atlanta is a regional bank and is part of the fifty-ninth largest bank holding company in the United States. The bank has been expanding recently, buying up other banks in the state.

First Atlanta's management associate development program, which lasts eighteen months to two years, is designed to meet the corporation's needs for management personnel in the trust, international, corporate banking, and metropolitan banking divisions. The bank hires 10 MBAs and 30 BAs per year. The program includes orientation to the bank, divisional rotations, credit analysis, and internships. During these various stages, a management advisor is available for career counseling.

After a week-long orientation period, designed to help associates become acquainted with the bank's senior management, trainees begin "modular training," or rotations in various divisions of the bank. The modules are mixed so that the associates will have exposure to several corporate areas. After completing several modules, each associate spends from six to nine months in credit analysis, receiving intensive credit training and working with lending officers throughout the bank. Associates also spend four to six months in an internship program in selected departments. These internships are designed to give each associate a longer learning and working experience in one particular area. Permanent placement is based on First Atlanta's needs as well as the desires of the trainee.

Salaries are in the range of $16,000 to $25,000. Benefits include major medical and dental coverage, life insurance, free checking, discounted personal loans, discounts on stock commissions, and limited tuition reimbursement. In addition to the standard benefits package, First Atlanta was one of the first institutions to offer on-site day care for children.

First Union National Bank
First Union Plaza
Charlotte, North Carolina 28288
(704) 374-3565

First Union National Bank is part of First Union Corporation, the forty-seventh largest bank holding company in the United States. The bank's major competitors are Wachovia Bank and North Carolina National Bank, both of which are substantially larger than First Union. The bank, however, has been extremely profitable in recent years and is growing fairly rapidly.

The bank offers entry-level opportunities and specially tailored training programs in a number of divisions: corporate lending, retail banking, Cameron-Brown (the largest mortgage banking firm in the Southeast), management (liability management and trading), First Union Commercial Corporation (asset-based lending), and trust. The bank hires 65 to 85 trainees a year; the breakdown between MBAs and BAs fluctuates. Most new hires start in June, although some additional recruiting is done throughout the year.

In addition to entry-level training, classes are offered intermittently in management and supervisory skills, sales training, and banking skills.

Salaries begin in the high teens for BAs and in the mid-twenties and up for MBAs, depending on work experience. Benefits include major medical and dental coverage, life insurance, preferred mortgage rates, free checking, credit cards, and a savings incentive plan.

First Wisconsin National Bank
777 East Wisconsin Avenue
Milwaukee, Wisconsin 53202
(414) 765-4246

First Wisconsin is part of the seventy-first largest bank holding company in the United States and is the largest bank in the state. First Wisconsin offers a formal thirteen-month rotational training program, which has been running for 30 years. According to the bank, over 75 percent of senior management has gone through it. About 25 trainees are hired each year, evenly divided between MBAs and BAs.

Each trainee is assigned to a sponsor, who is a senior officer of the organization. The program begins with a three-week stint in teller training. This is followed by a three-week rotation in bank operations, which focuses on computer operations, systems, programming, and check processing. During the next week, trainees move into real estate finance, where they evaluate mortgage applications and make individual loan presentations to a panel of bank officers. A four-week stint in consumer credit is next, followed by fourteen weeks in a branch, where trainees have their first customer contact. During the final phase, which takes place in the credit division, trainees undergo 26 weeks of number-crunching and credit analysis and make six presentations to a review committee of bank officers. Halfway through this last rotation, everyone is permanently placed. Officer titles are usually conferred within the next year.

Salary information was unavailable. Benefits include group medical coverage, life and disability insurance, pension program, thrift plan, profit sharing, consumer credit at preferential rates, and tuition reimbursement for approved studies.

Fleet National Bank
55 Kennedy Plaza
Providence, Rhode Island 02903
(401) 278-6000

Fleet National Bank is the main subsidiary of the Fleet Financial Group, a diversified financial services company that is the sixty-second largest bank holding company in the United States. The bank was founded in 1791 and is one of the oldest in the country, with over 200 offices around the world. It is the largest bank in Rhode Island.

Fleet offers entry-level training in a variety of areas, including lending, branch management, operations management, product management, auditing, and information management. Approximately 35 people, mostly BAs, were hired during the 1984 recruiting season. New hires in lending go through six to twelve months of training. From day one, trainees work very closely with account officers, doing credit work for them. They also take courses in accounting, commercial banking and lending, and bank products. After classes are over, trainees serve an internship to an account officer, providing research for customer calls and preparing business proposals and credit reviews. They are promoted to account officer as soon as they are judged capable of handling all responsibilities.

The branch management program combines on-the-job training with classroom sessions. Trainees work in the branches, acquainting themselves with such everyday functions as opening accounts, managing operations, and interviewing customers who want credit. They also take courses in credit analysis, commercial banking, and sales skills. The program lasts from four to six months.

Entry-level training in operations management, product management, auditing and information management is basically on the job. A technical background is not an absolute prerequisite in any of these areas; the bank will hire liberal arts majors and help them out with night school if necessary.

The bank would not disclose salary information. Benefits include major medical coverage, life insurance, free checking, reduced mortgage and personal loan rates, profit sharing, and 75 percent tuition reimbursement after six months.

Florida National Bank
P.O. Box 689
Jacksonville, Florida 32201
(904) 359-5111

Florida National Bank's training program can lead to one of two career paths: branch management or commercial lending. The program lasts approximately twelve to sixteen months and accepts around fifteen college graduate business majors per year. The major training tool is the Omega course, a programmed self-study instruction method (see the Pittsburgh National Bank listing for a full description). Trainees also have the opportunity to familiarize themselves with bank operations and customer service. After the program, trainees going to work in one of the bank's 135 branches find themselves taking on more and more lending responsibilities and less and less administrative work. Those going into commercial lending work with middle-market companies or perhaps in real estate lending, which is considered to be one of FNB's stronger activities.

The bank starts new employees at $15,000 to $16,000. Benefits include medical and dental coverage, life insurance, reduced origination rates for mortgages, profit sharing, and tuition reimbursement on a sliding scale depending on grades.

Goldome
One Fountain Plaza
Buffalo, New York 14203
(716) 847-5800

Goldome is one of the largest savings banks in the nation. It began as the Buffalo Savings Bank, but in the last few years it has made a number of acquisitions, including the New York Bank for Savings, which was New York State's oldest savings bank and, some say, the inventor of the passbook. As it expanded outside the greater Buffalo area, the bank changed its name to Goldome. Rapid expansion continues with the purchase of Bankers Trust's retail operations in the Albany area. Goldome also has a mortgage banking business that operates in six states.

Goldome's management development program hired approximately fifteen to twenty MBAs in 1982 and 1983 and six during 1984 who were interested in taking on a managerial position within the bank. Trainees begin with a hands-on rotation in the retail division that lasts about ten weeks. Then they move on to marketing/product development, where they work on developing new financial services and marketing them to the bank's customer base. Trainees also go through corporate planning to gain an overview of the organization and its strategic direction. They may also have a chance to work in Goldome Realty or another subsidiary of the bank. Following the rotations, trainees are asked to perform a practical exercise in the management of a particular function. On-the-job training is supplemented with seminars in corporate planning, personnel development, time management, sales, effective writing, and public speaking.

Goldome did not want to disclose salary information. Benefits include medical and disability insurance, incentive savings plan (available after six months), partial tuition reimbursement, free credit cards, free checks and traveler's checks, reduced interest rates on consumer loans and mortgages, and waiver of some closing costs on residential mortgages.

Interfirst Bank
P.O. Box 83120
Dallas, Texas 75283
(214) 744-7723

Interfirst is part of the sixteenth largest bank holding company in the United States. The bank has been having some financial problems recently because of the high losses they have taken on their energy loan portfolio.

Interfirst hires approximately 100 people a year, both BAs and MBAs, to take part in their credit training program. They hire four times a year and look for candidates with good analytical and marketing skills. The program lasts between one and one-and-a-half years and begins with a course in intermediate accounting taught by a professor on loan from Southern Methodist University. The class lasts for eight weeks and is taught by the case study method. In addition, the bank offers seminars on various bank products and services once or twice a week. These are given continuously throughout training and are led by department heads within the bank.

After the accounting class, trainees work in the credit department for six weeks, basically doing number-crunching. They then do five to six rotations that last six to eight weeks each through various bank departments, including energy, real estate, U.S. corporate banking, Dallas corporate banking, Metroplex (consumer and small business banking), and international banking. In conjunction with bank management, trainees then decide on the division that they would like to enter permanently. They then spend six months in this division as an intern. In this capacity, they perform backup work for a pool of officers and help prospect for new customers. During this period, trainees also go through seminars in basic sales and building business relationships. These classes are taught by in-house personnel. At the end of the six-month internship, trainees get their officer title and are given a portfolio of their own accounts.

The bank would not disclose salary or benefits information.

Irving Trust
One Wall Street
New York, New York 10015
(212) 487-2121

Irving Trust, named after the nineteenth-century American writer Washington Irving, is part of the twenty-second largest bank holding company in the United States. The bank considers itself in the forefront of correspondent banking—managing business relationships with other banks. Recently, it has also put together an investment banking group in an attempt to catch up with Bankers Trust and some of the other commercial banks that have become competitive in this area.

The bank hires BAs and MBAs at the entry level for placement in a number of different divisions, including corporate banking, international banking, trading, investment banking, personal banking, auditing, and operations. There are two structured training programs: one in credit and one in personal banking. Training for auditing and operations, which together hire about 65 people a year, is all on the job.

Between 50 and 100 trainees go through the credit program and are placed in the corporate, international, investment banking, or trading divisions. The program begins with seminars designed to familiarize new employees with the bank and to instruct them on what will be expected of them. Trainees also take a course in basic accounting that is held two afternoons a week for four weeks. Not everyone is required to take this course, but everyone must pass a test given at the end.

Once trainees have demonstrated a firm understanding of basic accounting principles, they participate in an advanced accounting course that lasts about eight weeks. Another important exam that must be passed is given at the conclusion of this course. Accounting is taught by professors from various business schools, including New York University and the University of Virginia.

Along with their coursework, trainees have on-the-job responsibilities, performing credit analyses to build on what they have learned in class. Seminars in banking and credit analysis are also given. This period of rather intensive credit training is followed by three rotations in different areas of the bank. Each rotation lasts from four to six weeks, and the area is determined by the trainee manager and the trainee. During this time, the training manager and a supervisor in one of the divisions evaluate the trainee's performance. The rotations are followed by a brief stint in operations and then permanent placement. No one is hired directly for a particular division because the bank feels it is better to give new people a well-rounded view of the organization.

Irving also runs a structured training program for personal bankers—bank representatives in branches who service up-scale retail customers. It is a much shorter program, lasting only six months, and covers many of the same areas as the credit training program, with additional emphasis on selling skills. Approximately ten people go through this program each year.

Irving hires both BAs and MBAs. Although accounting is not a prerequisite, candidates should be able to demonstrate strong quantitative skills. A transcript is also required. The attrition rate in Irving's programs is 15 percent to 20 percent, although it is not the bank's stated policy to overhire.

Starting salaries for BAs are between $22,000 and $24,000; for MBAs salaries range from $32,000 to $34,000. Benefits include major medical coverage, life insurance, and profit sharing.

Manufacturers Hanover Trust Company
320 Park Avenue
New York, New York 10022
(212) 644-7782

"Manny Hanny" is part of the fourth largest bank holding company in the nation, and it operates all over the globe. The bank recently purchased CIT Financial Corporation, a company engaged in consumer and middle-market financing, from RCA. The acquisition was the largest in the history of bank holding companies. Senior management at Manny Hanny is hopeful that the transaction will change the bank's image from that of a market follower to a definitive market leader.

The bank has a lending and credit training program, not only for future loan officers but also for other entry-level hires that provides trainees with a strong background in credit. The bank hires about 140 BAs and 60 MBAs a year and runs them through training in batches of 25 to 30 people. There are separate programs for BAs and MBAs. The number hired in a given year depends on how the bank and the economy are doing.

Trainees pretty much know where they will be going at the outset of the program. The sponsoring departments include international, national, corporate banking, and retail banking. Other departments that sponsor trainees through all or parts of the program are portfolio and investment banking division, Manufacturers Hanover Leasing Corporation, Manufacturers Credit Corporation, the real estate and mortgage division, and the cash management department. Trainees are hired into a specific division up front, and then that division sponsors them through the program.

Training begins with a management program seminar, which is an orientation to the banking industry and Manny Hanny. BA trainees then begin seven weeks of classes in accounting (from the basics to the not so basic) and money and banking. These courses are taught by outside professors. They then spend five weeks on the job, providing support to the division where they will eventually be placed. Next, they return to class again for seven weeks in corporate finance and business law, followed by a credit analysis seminar that lasts six weeks and is an extremely important part of the program. After successful completion of the credit analysis seminar, trainees for the national division, corporate banking division, and the retail banking division will be placed in their divisions. Those going into corporate banking will be assigned to a credit pool for a period of time where they will prepare loan reports and do number-crunching. After this period, they are assigned to a platform position in one of the lending centers. Those slated for the international division are not immediately assigned after the credit training program; rather they go on to a one-month seminar in international credit analysis and a nine-week rotation in the operations division. Those slated for the retail banking division are assigned to a branch as branch credit representatives, advising customers on their credit needs and marketing the bank's products. Staff members for the leasing department, real estate and mortgage department, and cash management department are also assigned to their divisions after the credit training program and begin to assume job responsibilities.

The program for MBAs lasts only eighteen weeks and consists of courses in accounting, finance, noncredit services, marketing, and credit analysis.

Trainees slated for the portfolio and investment banking division go through only the accounting, money and banking, and marketing courses of the credit training program. The rest of their time is spent rotating among different departments in the division, including money markets, government dealer, public finance, portfolio, and asset/liability management. Rotations last for one year, after which time trainees are permanently placed. The placement decision is based on where the trainee has demonstrated an aptitude and interest and where the bank has a need. Trainees for this division should have a background in economics, finance, accounting, and money and banking.

Trainees going into Manufacturers Hanover Commercial Corporation, in either asset-based lending or factoring, go through extensive on-the-job training in addition to the credit training program already discussed. All candidates for these areas should have a bachelor's degree in finance or accounting.

Asset-based lenders spend three to four months on the job before the credit training program begins. During this time, they are introduced to collateral* and credit analysis as well as to operational procedures within the division. In the third phase of the training program, which lasts four months, trainees go on calls with experienced officers in order to learn how to evaluate collateral. Trainees also begin to write loan proposals and make verbal credit presentations. Eventually they become responsible for managing their own accounts under the supervision of a senior lending officer.

Trainees going into the factoring division of Manufacturers

Hanover Commercial Corporation spend about six months rotating through the various functional areas—including collections, accounts receivable, and credit investigations—before they begin the credit training program. After the program, they spend about nine months as credit analysts, looking at client accounts for credit quality. Following this, they spend six months in the account executive area, which is the division where the officers are actually calling on customers. After three months in this division, the supervisor will make a determination as to whether or not the trainee will become a credit analyst or an account executive.

Trainees are, to a large extent, evaluated on the basis of exams given during classes. One Manny Hanny trainee told us that those who failed courses were out of the program. The people we talked to who had been through the program told us that about 20 percent didn't make it through. At Manny Hanny, at least, trainees know they aren't competing with one another for the same job because the bank's policy is not to hire unless a vacancy exists.

Salaries for BAs are in the range of $20,000 to $25,000 and MBAs start in the mid-thirties if they have two years of significant work experience, otherwise they get $28,000 to $30,000. Benefits include medical and partial dental insurance, reduced credit card and loan rates, free checking, and profit sharing. The bank has a formula line tuition reimbursement program—they pay 100 percent for As and Bs, 75 percent for a B− through a C−, and 50 percent for passing grades below a C−.

Marine Midland Bank
One Marine Midland Center
Buffalo, New York 14240
(716) 843-2424

140 Broadway
New York, New York
10015
(212) 440-1000

Marine Midland is majority-owned by the Hong Kong Shanghai Bank and is part of the fifteenth largest bank holding company in the nation. Although it is headquartered in Buffalo, Marine Midland has significant operations in New York City, so inquiries can also be addressed there. It is the largest retail bank in New York State.

The bank hires 25 people a year for its one-year management associate program. Of this amount, 80 percent to 90 percent are BAs, and the remainder are MBAs. All on-the-job management training takes place in the credit department. Trainees spend much of the time number-crunching and analyzing spread sheets* and credit in support of the lending officers. During this time, trainees work for four different supervisors for three months each. Classes, which are taught by bank officers as well as business school professors from New York University and the University of Virginia, are given in beginning, intermediate, and advanced accounting and in credit/financial analysis, money and banking, and loan documentation. Classes make up about 25 percent of the program. Briefings on the economy are also given about once a month. In addition, senior management makes presentations and trainees tour different bank areas.

Trainees who make it through the program are promoted to commercial bank representatives. Within two years of entering Marine Midland, trainees become first officers and may move into corporate/international banking, money management, credit policy, administration, or national banking. Trainees report that Marine offers good opportunities for advancement as well as a competitive but "comfortable" environment.

BAs start at a minimum of $22,500. MBAs start at $32,000 and up. Benefits include major medical and dental coverage, life insurance, profit sharing (after one year), and reduced loan rates (after six months).

Maryland National Bank
225 North Calvert Street
Baltimore, Maryland 21202
(301) 244-5000

The state's largest bank and part of the sixty-first largest bank holding company in the nation, Maryland National Bank has over 195 offices in Maryland, one in Washington, D.C., and 5 overseas. The bank is looking to expand its operations so it will be able to maintain its market share in the state. To this end, MNB has been adding branches and is interested in buying the Bank of Maryland.

The bank offers formal training programs in three different areas: commercial banking, auditing, and branch banking. In the commercial banking program, which lasts one year, trainees receive technical training in spreading financial statements and in cash-flow analysis. They help prepare actual analyses for presentation to, and review by, the loan committee.

The auditing program, which lasts one year, combines seminars and financial and operational audit assignments. The goal of the program is to train new hires in bank procedures, internal audit techniques, and operations. The branch banking program lasts one year and alternates classroom and departmental tours with on-the-job assignments emphasizing retail banking. It includes teller, customer account, installment lending, credit auditing, and bank operations training. Upon completion of the program, trainees join branch management and become responsible for profit planning, budgeting, and consumer and commercial lending, in addition to staff supervision and new business development.

Maryland National also offers entry-level positions in bank operations and data processing; training is basically all on the job.

The bank would not disclose salary information. Benefits include health and dental coverage, life insurance, profit sharing, tuition reimbursement, free checking, reduced credit card rates, and discounts on health clubs and travel packages.

Mellon Bank
Mellon Square
Pittsburgh, Pennsylvania 15230
(412) 232-4100

Mellon Bank is part of the thirteenth largest bank holding company in the country and is the biggest bank in Pennsylvania. It is sometimes considered the Morgan Guaranty of the regional banks because of its rather conservative, establishment reputation. According to industry surveys, Mellon's account officers are very well respected, and the bank's cash management products are considered excellent. Too bad it's in Pittsburgh, you say? Think again. Pittsburgh has been trying hard to spruce up its image. Pockets of trendiness are popping up all over, and there's even a neighborhood called Shady Side, where Yuppies are said to abound!

Mellon has been growing just like its archrival down the street, Pittsburgh National Bank. In 1982 Mellon bought Girard Bank in Philadelphia, Central Counties Bank, and Northwest Pennsylvania Corporation. Now it faces the hard task of integrating all these operations into the Mellon Bank culture. Mellon recruits for entry-level positions in a number of areas; training is primarily on the job. Corporate consulting, which provides market research, operations design, and other analytical services to Mellon as well as to other banks (for a fee), hires MBAs. The finance department, which advises bank senior management on day-to-day as well as long-term financial planning, also hires MBAs. The marketing and communications department, which handles advertising, marketing, and corporate communications, hires MBAs and people with experience in commercial design. Portfolio and funds management, the bank's trading operation, hires MBAs and BAs (with strong economics and/or math backgrounds). The trust department hires BAs (with accounting, economics, or finance) and MBAs. Finally, the community banking area (retail banking) hires BAs and MBAs. More formalized training is provided for those going into the national banking, credit policy, international, and information management divisions. New hires in lending areas usually have MBAs.

The national banking division consists of corporate lending, correspondent banking, and corporate services. Corporate lenders and correspondent bankers, as well as trainees from the credit policy area, participate in a formalized credit training program that begins with twelve to eighteen weeks of intensive study in courses ranging from credit analysis to loan documentation. After classes, corporate lenders spend from nine to twelve months as Mellon credit analysts, working on new credit proposals and tracking loan performance. They then do a stint in cash management, while the correspondent bankers start working. Training lasts about a year for MBAs and is somewhat longer for BAs.

Cash management products are one of Mellon's specialities, and new hires in this division are trained through a four-level program called Cash Management University. Level I, basic education, gives participants an overview of Mellon's organizational structure and of global cash management. Level II, product knowledge, covers such technical topics as automated clearinghouse, wire transfers, control disbursement, sweep accounts, corporate trade payments, zero balance accounts, and lockbox. In level III trainees spend time learning about other noncredit services offered by the bank, and in Level IV instruction is provided in sales and marketing techniques. Most new hires are MBAs.

The international division looks for MBAs, BAs, BSs, and those with master's degrees in international relations to take part in its management development training program, which includes classroom training and credit analysis of both multinational companies and international credits. Trainees may also be assigned to do special work in international economics, money desk (trading operations), planning and development, and international cash management.

Mellon's information management and research division provides systems and data processing support for the bank. BA and BS recruits take part in a formal training program that provides an overview of how the department functions as well as training in the technical programming skills required.

There is also a four-month training program in operations, the area that provides "back office" support to the bank's line areas. Trainees in this area spend some time in one of the branches and in money management.

The bank hires around 150 people per year. Starting salaries vary. The bank would not be specific about numbers, but discussions with trainees indicate that BAs start somewhere in the high teens to low twenties, with MBAs, starting in the high twenties to mid-thirties. Benefits include Blue Cross/Blue Shield, major medical and dental coverage, life insurance, long-term disability, cash award (half of one month's salary plus 5 percent of that amount for each year of service), profit sharing, thrift plan, free checking, special rates on bank services, and tuition reimbursement for courses that apply directly to the job.

Midlantic National Bank
Metro Park Plaza
Edison, New Jersey 08818
(201) 321-8000

East Coasters will probably recognize Midlantic. It's full of hungry bankers, or at least that's what the television ads say. Midlantic is the fifty-second largest bank in the United States and has a large branch network throughout New Jersey.

The bank has two training programs—one that it calls the "general" program and one in credit. The general program prepares four to six BAs and BSs a year for positions in the controller's office, the trust department, international operations, and the credit department. The program lasts a year.

The credit program takes six to eight BAs and BSs per year through an eighteen-month course designed to prepare them for positions in international banking, branch management, installment credit, loan review, and real estate. Trainees for both programs begin in July, when they attend three weeks of orientation. The seminars are taught by internal bank staff and cover the bank's products, services, and structure. After this, both groups of trainees spend three to four weeks in accounting and credit analysis courses. Subsequently, the two groups separate.

Generalists do rotations of six to twelve weeks, working on specific projects in the division to which they are assigned (one of the five mentioned earlier). After twelve months they are permanently placed in staff positions in one of these areas.

Lenders do three rotations, two lasting two months each and one lasting six months. The rotations take them through three of the five areas listed earlier, and they are later permanently placed in one of them. Rotations are supplemented with seminars designed to familiarize trainees with the bank's products and services. Following the rotations, trainees spend six months in the credit department, analyzing line cases and working directly with loan officers. Evaluations are based mainly on job performance rather than on classwork. After eighteen months, trainees move into loan officer slots, loan review, or loan supervision.

Salaries start at approximately $17,000. Benefits include major medical coverage, life insurance, reduced loan rates, and tuition reimbursement.

Morgan Guaranty
23 Wall Street
New York, New York 10004
(212) 483-2323

Morgan is part of the fifth largest bank holding company in the United States. Widely known as a conservative bank, Morgan's approach to its blue chip clients is successful, and the bank is one of the most envied and respected in the industry. Morgan does not have a major retail operation; it caters only to individuals with assets greater than $2 million as well as to corporations and governments.

Morgan's commercial banking management program is widely regarded as one of the best and most demanding in the industry. High-level Morgan bankers usually start with the firm, which has a lower degree of turnover than most other banks. This loyalty helps to support management's espoused philosophy of teamwork.

The commercial banking program is run three times a year —in July, October, and January—and consists of three phases lasting three months each. Each cycle has from 45 to 50 participants, some of whom have MBAs. One unique aspect of Morgan's training is that almost half of the training group consists of foreign nationals hired by overseas branches.

BAs participate in all three program phases; MBAs go through only the last two. Phase I consists of courses in basic accounting, introductory economics, and corporate finance. Two three-hour classes are held each day, usually in different subjects. In some cases, outside professors are brought in. In order to have some time to prepare homework assignments, trainees are given two independent study and preparation sessions per week. Participants report that they often have to spend at least two hours a night on take-home assignments. Exams are administered at the end of the courses and are used in the initial evaluation of trainees.

MBAs join the BAs in Phase II of the program, which is much more rigorous than Phase I. Classroom sessions cover advanced accounting and credit analysis, followed by a short course on international economics. During this period, officers from different areas within the bank participate in workshops designed to introduce trainees to areas they may want to consider for assignment after the program is completed.

Phase III of the program is spent in the financial analysis division. This is the most technical and, some say, the most tedious portion of the program. Trainees are required to use the skills learned in Phases I and II to analyze three companies in the same detail as an account officer would. The results of individual cases are reviewed by line officers. At the end of Phase III trainees are assigned to specific areas in the bank for two-year posts.

Trainees can go into a variety of areas, from corporate foreign exchange advisory services to correspondent banking and corporate lending. The bank tries to accommodate trainees' first choices. Overall, there is not a heavy emphasis on placing all trainees in lending positions even though they have the requisite training.

BAs start at approximately $24,000, with a raise after about six months. MBAs start at $35,000 or more, depending on school and work experience. Benefits include medical and dental coverage, life insurance, profit sharing, reduced commissions on stock transactions, and limited tuition reimbursement.

NCNB National Bank of North Carolina
One NCNB Plaza
Charlotte, North Carolina, 28255
(704) 374-5000

NCNB has been characterized as the most aggressive bank holding company in the Southeast. In the past two years, it has bought five Florida banks in an attempt to keep the money center banks from monopolizing the profitable Florida market. And in the process it has become the twenty-fifth largest in the United States. The bank has over 500 domestic offices and international operations in six foreign countries.

NCNB recruits primarily in the Southeast, but also covers the East Coast schools. The bank seeks to attract the best candidates possible, and it is willing to pay for them. For this reason, NCNB's starting salaries may be just as good as those offered by a major money center bank. And since the cost of living in North Carolina is undoubtedly lower than in the major money centers, NCNB bankers can afford to live pretty well.

The lending officer program lasts for nine to twelve months, depending on the individual candidate. The bank hires around 80 BAs (with some accounting background) and MBAs per year. For three to six months trainees work for an account officer, analyzing financial statements in cases ranging from international credits to middle-market lending. After this, trainees spend nine weeks in full-time classes taught by senior management of the bank. Here the emphasis is again on credit, but courses also cover product knowledge and selling skills. Trainees then return to the credit department and await permanent placement. There are two routes to take. Trainees who want careers with Fortune 500 companies will be based in North Carolina and will travel fairly extensively. Trainees who want to work with smaller companies will be based either in North Carolina or Florida (a decision made at the end of the program).

The funds management program prepares candidates for positions as either traders or salespeople. About five people, usually MBAs, are hired into this area each year. Training involves six to nine months of rotations, after which a decision is made on permanent placement. At NCNB, traders and salespeople are rewarded on the basis of their team's performance rather than individually. This policy, according to sources within the company, makes the atmosphere a little less tense than that typically found in a trading room.

The trust department program lasts about two months and consists of seminars with the major heads of the trust division and short rotations among three areas in trust—new business, operations, and investment management. This division takes approximately ten people a year, mostly with MBAs.

The operations and accounting areas take about twenty and ten people per year respectively, most of whom are BAs. All training is on the job, but newcomers are exposed to senior management through a series of seminars held at the bank's headquarters.

Salaries start in the upper teens for BAs and from the mid-twenties to low thirties for MBAs. Benefits include major medical plan, group life insurance, stock thrift plan, and tuition reimbursement if classes relate to employment.

National City Corporation
1900 East 9th Street
Cleveland, Ohio 44114
(216) 575-2000

National City, a Midwestern regional bank headquartered in Cleveland, is part of the forty-eighth largest bank holding company in the United States. With approximately 160 offices in the state, it is the second largest bank in Ohio, after BancOne; but like many regional banks it is looking to expand and attain enough market share to make it difficult for the money center banks to invade the state. The bank has undertaken a number of acquisitions in recent years and is currently attempting to acquire BankOhio. If the acquisition goes through, National City will be the largest bank in the state.

The bank runs two training programs a year: one for BAs and one for MBAs. Approximately 25 BAs and 12 MBAs are hired. Major recruiting activities take place at universities in Ohio, Indiana, Michigan, and Western Pennsylvania.

The training program for BAs leads to an assistant manager position in a branch. BAs are expected to have a business major, or at least some accounting and finance courses. The bank does not have a structured classroom training program. Instead, BAs are given a counselor within the bank and are then sent out to branches to work in what is essentially a big brother/big sister program. The counselor is not associated with the trainee's branch and thus can offer objective advice.

BAs are trained to be generalists. First, they spend about nine months in the branch with duties that include those of teller, head teller, and third desk (assisting the branch's assistant manager). At this time, the branch manager may take the trainee out on customer calls. Later, trainees go to the bank's headquarters, where they work rotations in consumer credit, credit and operations, real estate mortgages, and the trust department. After these rotations, trainees return to the branch as assistant managers. After four to six months, trainees are given some lending authority and begin making small loans. Approximately nine months to a year later, trainees work a six-month stint in the credit department. Here, they perform in-depth analyses of companies' financial statements. The objective of this phase is to get trainees to develop the ability to think independently.

The MBA program is designed to produce corporate lending officers. There are three rotational assignments, one each in the credit, product management, and investment divisions. After two and a half years of rotations and three to six months in a calling relationship with a senior account officer, the MBA is assigned to a particular territory and gains responsibility for existing account relationships as well as new business development in this area. In each rotation, both MBAs and BAs are assigned to one supervisor who evaluates their performance verbally and in writing after the rotation is over.

National City offers salaries of $16,000 to $18,000 for BAs and $25,000 for MBAs. Benefits include major medical and dental coverage, life insurance, reduced loan rates—including on mortgages, free checking, tuition reimbursement, and reduced credit card rates.

NatWest USA
44 Wall Street
New York, New York 10005
(212) 623-4000

NatWest, formerly the National Bank of North America, was acquired in 1979 by a British bank, National Westminster PLC. It is currently among the fifty largest banks in the

United States. NatWest is trying to set up loan production offices in major U.S. cities. In terms of corporate lending, the bank considers its strong points to be in cable television and health care.

NatWest offers a training program for 25 to 35 BAs and MBAs a year who are interested in becoming corporate lending officers; 85 percent of entering trainees are BAs. The program is run in three divisions—U.S. corporate, international, and Greater New York (middle-market lending)—and lasts sixteen to eighteen months. Training is 60 percent on the job and 40 percent in the classroom.

Training begins with a four-month course in accounting, that moves from the basics to more advanced topics. Tests and case studies are used to judge trainees' competency. Trainees report that the course is comprehensive and fairly difficult and requires at least one to two hours of homework every night.

The remainder of training consists of three or four four-month rotations within the division in which the trainee was hired. During this phase, participants spend four days on the job and one day in class. On-the-job duties consist of backup account officer work, which includes a great deal of number-crunching. Trainees attend classes in corporate finance, macroeconomics, and money and banking and a series of seminars on the bank's products.

Salaries for BAs begin at $21,000; MBAs come in at $32,000. According to trainees, even though these salary levels may be somewhat lower than what the competition offers, NatWest increases them substantially after promotion. Benefits include major medical and dental coverage, life insurance, reduced-rate loans, reduced commissions on stock transactions, discount credit card rates, tuition reimbursement, and a savings incentive plan (the bank matches up to 6 percent of salary).

Philadelphia National Bank
Broad and Chestnut Streets
Philadelphia, Pennsylvania 19101
(215) 629-3100

A regional bank, Philadelphia National services individuals and medium-size and large corporations in its market area, which includes the mid-Atlantic region.

The bank runs a wholesale banking training program three times a year—in March, June, and October. The program, which lasts a total of eighteen months, accepts 25 trainees (BAs and MBAs) each year. When they join the bank, trainees are assigned a sponsor who is a senior officer of the bank but who is not their boss. The sponsor is there for advice and guidance during the training program.

The program begins with a seven-week class in accounting and an introduction to corporate finance. Classes are taught by 25 line officers who give presentations in their areas of expertise. Afterward, trainees are assigned two six-month stints as credit analysts. During this period, trainees basically shadow account managers, usually in large corporate lending or a specialty area, going on calls and working on marketing strategies with them. Performance during this period directly influences where the trainee will be permanently placed. While working as credit analysts, trainees also take courses one day a week in corporate finance and financial analysis. These courses are taught by professors from the University of Pennsylvania's Wharton School. Trainees also have to make presentations of their own credit analyses to a mock loan committee.

Following the two rotations as credit analysts, trainees go on a six-month marketing tour in cash management. They begin with six to seven weeks of training in operations and product knowledge and take a sales course taught by an outside consultant. Trainees are then given the opportunity to apply what they have learned in a four-month rotation in both domestic and international cash management. Here they put together proposals and start to call on customers on their own as product specialists.

Following this, trainees are promoted to line assignments in one of six wholesale areas: regional banking, large corporate banking, specialized industry banking, correspondent banking, community banking, and corporate banking services.

BAs start at around $17,000, with MBAs starting in the mid-twenties. Trainees who perform well during the training program can receive raises every six months. Benefits include major medical and dental coverage, life insurance, and reduced loan rates.

Pittsburgh National Bank
Pittsburgh National Building
Pittsburgh, Pennsylvania 15265
(412) 355-2666

Pittsburgh National Bank is part of the PNC Financial Corporation, the twenty-seventh largest bank holding company in the United States. The holding company was formed in January 1983 when Pittsburgh National Bank bought Provident National Bank in Philadelphia. With some 116 branches, PNB is a very profitable bank and has been showing some very attractive measures of return on assets and return on equity. The bank may very well start giving Mellon a run for its money.

PNB runs two training programs: one for community (branch) banking and one for corporate lending. Each year five to ten BAs, generally with a background in accounting, enter the program for community banking. Trainees spend three months each in two branches, getting oriented to branch operations and helping wherever they can. They are then sent to headquarters for a six-month stint that includes two months in the Omega program—a training tool designed by a consulting firm in California to teach credit analysis for commercial lending decisions. A pretest is given on the assumption that the trainee already has a good background in accounting and finance. Trainees spend half the day in classes and half the day doing homework. After their stay at headquarters, trainees go out for three more branch rotations—the first two for three months each and the last one for six months. By the time they are done with the program, trainees will have been in five branches and seen five different management styles. After each stay, the trainee's performance is evaluated. It takes approximately two years to make branch assistant manager.

PNB's corporate banking management training program is designed to train individuals for positions in three divisions—corporate lending, international, and credit. Trainees may know which of these three areas they are going into, but if they are entering corporate lending they won't know the specific department within it. Approximately fifteen to twenty trainees begin with the Omega program, which they attend with the community banking people. This is followed by two weeks of international credit analysis. Those going into the corporate or credit areas then spend a week in one of the branches, meeting people and getting a good feel for the products and services offered (mortgages, car loans, personal loans, and so on). The purpose here is to give line officers a broad range of knowledge so that when they go out to call on a corporate treasurer they can talk about the mortgage on the treasurer's house as well as lines of credit.

Trainees then spend from six to nine months as credit analysts, performing such duties as assessing risk and analyzing companies for creditworthiness. Trainees must demonstrate technical competence and are required to participate in a mock loan presentation to the credit staff and other trainees. At this time, individuals slated for the corporate division should be deciding into which of the divisions—multinational, commercial, merchant * (investment banking products)—they will be going. Trainees do not leave the credit department until they are judged ready and able. The bank is flexible in this regard. Some trainees have left after two months, while others remain for a year. Those going into the international division do not go to the branch but are assigned to the bank's economics department, where they perform risk assessments on different countries. Those going into the commercial or multinational division go through a one- to five-month rotation in cash management, during which time they make their first customer calls. Permanent placement is determined by three factors: (1) how well a trainee has done (based on regular evaluations), (2) where the trainee is needed, and (3) the personalities involved. It takes two and a half to three years to move from bank representative to bank officer.

PNB offers starting salaries of $22,000 for BAs and from $28,000 to $30,000 for MBAs. Benefits include major medical and dental coverage, life insurance, profit sharing (after six years) pension plan, reduced loan rates, stock purchase program, three quarters of market rate on credit cards, free checking, and 100 percent prepaid tutition for job-related courses if grades are acceptable; otherwise employee must reimburse bank.

Rainier National Bank
1301 5th Avenue
P.O. Box 3966
Seattle, Washington 98124
(206) 621-4111

Rainier is part of the fifty-third largest bank holding company in the United States and, along with Seafirst, is one of the two major banks in Washington State. Rainier has 214 offices throughout the state.

The bank hires twelve MBAs and BAs per year. Its credit training program lasts eighteen months and consists of three intense, highly structured phases. In Phase I, trainees go through three months of academic training spending approximately 30 hours per week in the classroom. The rest of their time is devoted to completing homework assignments. Trainees go through a graduate-level accounting course, the Omega program (see the Pittsburgh National Bank listing for a description), and additional courses in principles of banking, business law, economics, international banking, financial statement analysis, real estate lending, and written communications skills.

Tests and papers are assigned during this time. Phase II, which is nine months long, consists of departmental internships in both the retail and lending areas, each lasting one to four weeks. Subsequently, trainees go through four weeks of intensive orientation to the retail side of the bank while attending short seminars (from one hour to two days in length). The last part of this phase consists of seven weeks of one-on-one credit presentations. Trainees prepare one or two cases each week, and each presentation is reviewed by a line officer. Trainees then spend seven weeks with a different credit administrator, doing one or two cases each week. Phase II concludes with three short rotations—two weeks in credit evaluation, two weeks with a senior credit officer, and three and a half weeks in credit examination.

Phase III consists of three internships—each lasting two months—in the retail, wholesale, and international divisions. At this time, trainees do backup work for line officers and go on calls. After rotations, trainees are permanently assigned to one of these three areas. Promotion to officer title comes six to ten months after Phase III, depending on performance. Surprisingly enough, given the rigorous nature of this program, the attrition rate is extremely low.

The bank would not disclose salary information, although they did claim to be competitive in their marketplace. Benefits include major medical and dental coverage, vision care plan, life insurance, free checking, reduced Visa fees and rates, tuition reimbursement, stock purchase plan, and a thrift plan.

Seattle First National Bank
10010 4th Avenue
Seattle, Washington 98214
(206) 583-3131

Seattle First National Bank, or Seafirst, as it is commonly known, is a wholly owned subsidiary of the BankAmerica Corporation. BAC took over in 1983, when Seafirst was having some trouble, primarily because of heavy energy loan exposure and the recession, which hit the Pacific Northwest particularly hard. On its own, Seafirst is the largest bank in Washington State, with over 150 offices and 7,000 employees.

Seafirst has a unique and very stringent screening process. Applicants whose résumés look attractive are given the opportunity to make a three-minute presentation in front of a committee. The topic: themselves. Those who pass this stage are required to take a three-hour accounting exam (at a later date) before being granted a half-hour interview. Despite this rigorous process, the bank does manage to hire around 40 people per year, a third of whom have MBAs.

Seafirst has two training programs: the bank officer candidate program and an EDP program. The bank officer program lasts one year and combines both operations and credit training. It is separated into four quarters, two in class and two on the job. The first quarter is spent in what Seafirst calls "bank management school." Classes are taught in Seattle, primarily by in-house personnel. Topics covered include an introduction to commercial banking and Seafirst and management skills. The program stresses the sales and marketing aspects of today's banking environment and includes a lengthy course on effective business presentations. During this time, participants make up to a dozen presentations, some of them videotaped, and are evaluated by peers and instructors. Exams are administered periodically.

The second quarter is spent in on-the-job training at one of Seafirst's branches. (During this phase, the bank tries to accommodate the trainee's preference for location.) Trainees are assigned mentors in the branches who are responsible for their progress. Initial assignments are usually in operations, where new hires are exposed to virtually all banking activities, from managing tellers to collecting installment loans.

In the third quarter, trainees return to the classroom for bank credit training. Accounting principles and corporate finance courses are provided to build a strong foundation in financial analysis. The classes are supplemented by presentations in commercial loan documentation and the operational aspects of lending. In this phase, trainees review the entire process of making a loan, and at the end they present case studies to the group and to line officers.

The last quarter of the program is held in a branch, usually not the same one as in Phase II. Once again trainees are assigned a mentor, this time a line lending officer in either personal loans or business loans. Trainees assist their bosses in preparing loan documentation and going on business development calls. At the conclusion of the program, trainees are promoted to the officer level and are assigned to a two-year post. Statewide mobility is a must, and almost all officers find themselves in one of the branches.

BAs at Seafirst start at $15,500 and MBAs at $24,000. Benefits include medical, dental, and vision coverage, life insurance, matched savings plan, banking services at reduced rates, subsidized busing transportation to and from work, and tuition reimbursement (50 percent after two years' employment with the bank).

Security Pacific National Bank
333 South Hope Street
Los Angeles, California 90071
(213) 613-6211

Security Pacific is part of the ninth largest bank holding company in the United States and has been one of the most profitable banks in the country over the past few years. The bank operates about 600 branches in California and regional offices throughout the country. It also has offices in over 23 countries overseas.

The bank has four separate training programs: for branch operations, commercial lending, world banking, and executive interns. Its philosophy is to promote people from within whenever possible, but at the entry level they do hire MBAs and BAs each year.

The branch program is run four times a year and lasts from six to seven months. This is the bank's largest training program. Trainees spend 80 percent of their time on the job, working in the branches and getting involved in daily activities, and 20 percent of their time in class, learning management skills and mastering the bank's products and services. After the training period is over, candidates are promoted to operations supervisors.

The commercial lending program was just started in 1983 and takes both BAs and MBAs. The program, which lasts about twelve months, consists of backing up middle-market lending officers and participating in workshops. Candidates also go through operations and consumer credit training. After completing the program, trainees are promoted to commercial lending officer.

The most competitive program is world banking, which is run once a year in Los Angeles. The program, which takes in MBAs and BAs, lasts one year for MBAs and two years for BAs. Trainees are given self-study assignments in analyzing credit needs, reducing credit risk, pricing credits/profitability analysis, foreign financial accounting, international loan types, business development, and management skills. On the job, trainees analyze credit requests and provide backup credit analyses for line officers. Trainees are evaluated at the end of the program through a credit presentation made to senior management.

The bank also runs an executive intern program for a very select group of MBAs. This two-year program consists of four six-month assignments with senior managers of the bank. Interns work on a series of projects ranging from analysis of executive transportation (a topic taken straight from the bank's brochure) to acquisition strategies. In addition, interns may take part in some aspects of the bank's officer training programs. At the conclusion of the program, interns are placed in managerial positions in an area where they have shown particular interest during their rotational assignments.

The bank would not disclose salaries and benefits information.

State Street Bank
225 Franklin Street
Boston, Massachusetts 02101
(617) 786-3000

State Street is an old-style New England bank whose primary business is providing commercial banking services to middle-market customers throughout the region. It is part of the eighty-third largest bank holding company in the nation. The highly profitable relationships State Street has developed and nurtured over the years still contribute significantly to the bank's bottom line. The bank, however, is currently trying to

113

downplay these "cash cows" and to establish new relationships, especially in the high-tech sector, an industry that in recent years has taken off in the Boston area.

State Street has had limited hiring needs recently, usually accepting only a few management trainees per year. Hiring represents about 1 percent to 2 percent of the applicant pool. In spite of this, the bank has a highly structured training program that has been in place since 1975. The program consists of two phases and combines classroom and on-the-job training. It lasts from 15 to 20 months for MBAs and 23 to 32 months for BAs.

Phase I begins in the bank's credit analysis unit. Trainees start as generalists, preparing analyses and presentations on bank customers and prospects. They often present their conclusions to a group of officers and other credit analysts, as though they were actual proposals being made internally, or to customers. The emphasis during this period is on actual job experience, supplemented by in-house seminars on bank products and services, loan documentation procedures, and various accounting topics of current interest. The more formal classroom training includes a course formulated by an outside vendor called "Commercial Loans to Business," which covers credit analysis and sales skills as they apply to lending. Short courses are also held in accounting and finance.

Phase II of the program is an on-line assignment as a senior credit analyst. Trainees continue to provide numerical analyses as in Phase I, but on a more sophisticated level. They assume greater responsibilities and start working directly with lending officers. Trainees assist officers in structuring call programs and make calls with the loan officer. Senior credit analysts are also given formal sales training in conjunction with increased customer contact. Before getting promoted to loan officer, trainees must make presentations to a committee that assesses their credit and sales skills.

The bank would not disclose salary information. Benefits include major medical and dental coverage, life insurance, free checking, and reduced rate personal loans.

Texas American Bank/Forth Worth
P.O. Box 2050
Fort Worth, Texas 76113
(817) 338-8191

Texas American Bank/Fort Worth is the flagship bank of Texas American Bancshares, Inc., the sixty-seventh largest bank holding company in the nation. It controls over twenty member banks throughout Texas.

The bank offers a commercial banking and business development program that lasts from twelve to eighteen months. Trainees start out with a one-week orientation session and then move to the credit department, which is where most training takes place. New hires rotate through different areas of the credit department, including the specialized loan group, the commercial loan group, and the national accounts/correspondent banking group. After nine months, they become senior analysts in one of these three areas. Senior credit analysts work closely with loan officers and do some calling with them. A number of analysts also participate in the loan assistant program, in which they are assigned for one or two months, to cash management, loan review, or other areas. During this time, they must continue to perform analyses for the credit department.

After the training program, many opportunities are open to the trainee. Final placement may be in corporate banking (which includes commercial, agriculture, petroleum, and real estate), national accounts (Fortune 500 companies), correspondent banking, international banking, or cash management. Trainees may also be placed in professional and executive banking, a new area for the bank that services professionals and high-net-worth individuals.

Salaries start in the low twenties for BAs and between $25,000 and $30,000 for MBAs. Benefits include medical and dental coverage, life insurance, profit sharing (five-year vesting period), free checking, preferential rates on credit cards, and tuition reimbursement based on grades.

Texas Commerce Bank
712 Main Street
P.O. Box 2558
Houston, Texas 77001
(713) 236-4865

Texas Commerce Bank is part of Texas Commerce Banc-shares, which is the twentieth largest bank holding company in the United States, with 65 member banks throughout Texas. On its own, TCB is one of the largest banks in the state.

The bank runs a commercial banking officer training program for approximately 40 to 50 people a year. Most new hires begin in either January or May and generally have MBAs. The program lasts for nine to twelve months and is mostly on the job. Trainees begin as credit analysts and provide backup analytical work for the five lending areas in the bank: middle market, large corporates, international, real estate, and energy. The bank also provides numerous short seminars, each lasting about three hours, on technical banking topics and credit skills. These seminars are taught by in-house personnel. Outside professors are brought in to instruct new trainees in banking law and loan documentation. Additionally, trainees must present two credit cases to the bank's loan committee. After the training period, new hires are permanently placed in one of the five areas discussed earlier.

Salaries for BAs begin at $17,000 to $19,000, with MBAs starting from $25,000 to $30,000. Benefits include major medical and dental coverage, life insurance, reduced loan rates, and credit card discounts.

Union Bank
445 South Figueroa
Los Angeles, California 90071
(213) 236-5000

Union Bank is headquartered in Los Angeles and has branches throughout California. It is a part of Standard Chartered Bank Group, a British bank with a network of 1,900 offices in 63 countries. On its own, Union Bank is the thirty-eighth largest bank in the nation.

The bank runs major training programs in the auditing and lending areas. The auditing program accepts candidates with BSs in business, preferably with a concentration in accounting. Candidates should have at least an intermediate accounting course and a firm grasp of statistics and business law. Training is essentially on the job and consists of rotations through the various functional areas of the auditing department.

There are two programs offered in the lending area. Both are account management programs and require an undergraduate or graduate degree in business, accounting, economics, or finance. One of the programs, a nonaccelerated course, is available to MBAs, BAs or BSs with minimal work experience but with at least one year of accounting. The program lasts twenty months, and the bank takes 32 people a year. The accelerated program lasts only twelve months and is offered to BSs with two years of related work experience or to MBAs with a year of related work experience. There are approximately 32 people in the accelerated program in any given year. Both the accelerated and nonaccelerated programs combine intensive classroom instruction with on-the-job training. Final placement may be in any one of a number of areas, including asset-based financing, corporate banking, international banking, and real estate lending.

Salaries start at $18,000 for the nonaccelerated program and $23,000 for the accelerated program. Benefits include medical and dental coverage, vision care, life insurance, investment plan, and discounts on selected bank services.

U.S. Trust
45 Wall Street
New York, New York 10005
(212) 806-4500

Founded in 1853, U.S. Trust offers a wide range of investment and trust services to corporations and individuals. The bank's traditional strength has been in personal trust management, but now it is also moving into money management. The company operates two offices in New York and one in Palm Beach. The Florida office was recently permitted to accept consumer deposits, a step considered to be one more move by the Federal Reserve toward interstate banking.

U.S. Trust offers a training program in its personal asset management division for a handful of MBAs and/or BSs in finance who have coursework in security analysis or portfolio management. The program, which lasts a year, combines classroom and on-the-job training. The first class, an introduction to U.S. Trust, includes seminars with managers of the firm. Further workshops are provided in personal financial planning, sales development, and effective communications skills. While in training, candidates are assigned to a senior portfolio manager whom they assist in managing clients' portfolios. They also learn the basics of securities analysis from the research department, where they are assigned on a temporary basis. Within three years, trainees should be handling their own accounts.

The bank would not disclose salary information. Benefits include profit sharing and tuition reimbursement.

Valley National Bank
P.O. Box 71
Phoenix, Arizona 85001
(602) 261-2900

Valley National Bank is part of the thirty-sixth largest bank holding company in the United States and is the largest bank in Arizona. It is a regional bank serving retail and commercial customers through 200 offices located across the state. Valley currently employs over 6,500 people in its branch system and fills most branch lending and management track positions with entry-level BAs. There are four distinct programs for both entry-level trainees and in-house employees.

Two training programs are offered at the branch level: branch operations and branch credit. For the past year, in-house personnel have been hired for this program, although the bank was unsure whether this trend would continue in the future. Both programs train generalists to work in Valley's branch network, but they offer distinct career paths. The operations management program prepares employees to oversee operations personnel in their everyday functions and to answer directly to branch managers. The program lasts from twelve to sixteen months (all Valley training programs are geared toward the individual's ability to advance) and consists almost entirely of on-the-job training. Areas covered include accounting, bookkeeping, teller duties, and accounts management. Candidates who successfully complete the program are assigned to specific branches as entry-level operations officers.

The branch, or consumer, credit program lasts twelve months and consists almost entirely of on-the-job training. Trainees begin with a brief assignment in the operations area at a branch and then go on to retail lending with a heavy emphasis on procedural routine. Toward the end of training they are assigned to back up a loan officer in the branch. Job responsibilities include all phases of booking* consumer loans, from interviewing potential borrowers to collecting loan payments. After completing training, participants are promoted to platform lending officers.

Valley has a strong agricultural loan portfolio—the bank accounts for nearly half of Arizona's agricultural lending. The bank offers a specific training program for officer candidates whose education and work experience combine finance or business with agriculture. Many candidates have degrees in agribusiness, for example. The program lasts from nine to twelve months and begins with an introduction to branch operations, supplemented by intensive individual and in-class study of agricultural lending. Areas stressed include internal credit procedures, lending policies, credit analysis, loan structuring, and lending documentation. The next phase is a specialized lending assignment that consists of backing up two or three line officers for two to three months each. These rotations are designed to give credit trainees exposure to the different elements of agricultural lending.

After training is completed, most trainees are transferred to the bank's state and southern divisions, where the major concentration of Arizona's agricultural lending is based. The usual initial position is branch lending officer, but some positions are also available in the headquarters' agribusiness loan department or the agricultural field section.

Valley's fastest-track program is in corporate credit training. About ten to twelve people, mostly MBAs, are hired to start in either June or January. Many officers who move into positions of management responsibility at Valley go through this program. It is the most structured and the longest of the programs offered, lasting from 18 to 24 months. Training begins with a formal six-month introduction to the bank's organization and branch operations. The operations phase is similar to the initial phase of the branch operations program, in which on-the-job training is supplemented by workshops and seminars. The next phase is spent in the headquarters' credit department and generally lasts six months, during which time trainees are given an in-depth exposure to commercial credit analysis and investigations. The primary component of this training is a seven-week advanced credit class taught by in-house instructors that covers advanced accounting, corporate finance, and credit case studies. On-the-job training includes locating and analyzing credit information for loan officers.

After commercial credit training, participants work in the credit evaluation section of the bank's auditing department in order to improve their working knowledge of loan procedures and auditing methods. The assignment is followed by six months of "live" training during which trainees are assigned to specific loan officers, assume daily office responsibilities, and are given the opportunity to start calling on customers. As the program ends, trainees are interviewed by various divisions for their first permanent assignment, which is decided by combining the bank's needs with the trainees' individual interests. Assignments can be anywhere in the state.

Salaries for MBAs start between $20,000 and $28,000 depending on work experience. Benefits include major medical and dental coverage, life insurance, disability pay, savings investment plan, reduced loan rates, and pension plan.

Wells Fargo Bank
475 Sansome Street
San Francisco, California 94163
(415) 396-0123

Wells Fargo is part of the twelfth largest bank holding company in the nation and has almost 400 branches across California. At present, Wells is making an effort to expand its middle-market and real estate operations in the state.

The bank has a credit management training program that hires MBAs or internal staff. There is no entry-level program for BAs without prior work experience, but new BAs can join the bank, spend some time number-crunching and making credit analyses, and then enter the program later on. New hires come in without a specific job and are placed after completing the program.

Training lasts nine to twelve months and is run in two sessions, one beginning in the spring and one beginning in late summer. It opens with an overview of the bank and the industry and continues with short rotations through the bank's branch network. This is followed by classroom training in uniform credit analysis, which covers the bank's methodology for risk evaluation and credit decision making. This part of the program lasts for ten weeks and is taught through case studies.

Trainees are given five to seven live credit cases on Fridays and must present them to the class on Mondays. According to trainees, it is futile to make weekend plans during this period. Before and after the uniform credit analysis course, trainees also attend seminars taught by consultants and Stanford University professors on bank accounting, micro- and macroeconomics, money markets and capital markets, sales training, and negotiation skills. Promotion comes at the end of the program, but the first raise is usually given about twelve months after joining. Most trainees are promoted to assistant vice president one-and-a-half to two years after coming on line.

Trainees report starting salaries of between $25,000 and $30,000. Benefits include major medical and dental coverage, life insurance, profit sharing (after three years), employee

121

stock option plan (after one year), reduced loan rates, reduced credit card rates, reduced commissions on stock transactions, and tuition reimbursement.

The World Bank
1818 H Street NW
Washington, D.C. 20433
(202) 477-1234

The World Bank has essentially three functions: lending money to, providing advice to, and stimulating investment interest in developing nations. There are three divisions within the bank: the International Bank for Reconstruction and Development (IBRD), the International Development Association (IDA), and the International Finance Corporation (IFC). The IBRD makes loans at a profit to the governments of developing nations, while the IFC lends money at a concessionary interest rate. The IDA lends money to corporations at commercial interest rates. The IBRD funds its loans through the subscriptions of its member nations, which include virtually all countries in the world except the Soviet Union and its allies. It also borrows money in the open market, much like a commercial bank. The IDA funds loans through grants from richer nations, while the IFC gets money through its member nations as well as from the IBRD.

Every year, the World Bank hires between 20 and 30 people to take part in its Young Professionals (YP) Program. The program is strictly on the job and consists of two or three rotations through the support, financial, and research areas of the bank. In the support area, YPs may be involved in organization and planning, personnel, or the controller's office. In financial, YPs work on feasibility studies for specific development projects within a particular industry. In research, YPs write economic reports on specific countries and compile projections on expected developments. YPs are not assigned to specific supervisors, but after the rotations, which last anywhere from a year to a year and a half, YPs are assigned to regular staff positions. During the rotations, they also attend a number of seminars given by bank staff to further acquaint them with the different functions within the organization.

The organizational structures within the World Bank have been described as "flat," and there is very little staff turnover. Generally, the job hierarchy is YP, economist, senior economist, division chief, assistant director, director. YPs, however, do get promoted, and at present there are quite a few former YPs at the assistant director and director levels.

Most candidates have advanced degrees in economics, international affairs, or business. Language skills are definitely a plus. Many YPs are foreign nationals living in the United States.

Salaries start at between $29,000 and $37,000 (net of taxes). Benefits information was unavailable.

5

Investment and Securities Houses

First Boston, Goldman Sachs, Lehman Brothers, Morgan Stanley, Salomon Brothers—these are just a few of the names associated with the biggest deals on The Street,* the biggest deals in America. They are the New York investment banks, homes to some of the most lucrative and exciting money jobs in the world. When the world's largest corporations contemplate major new financing strategies, they usually consult their investment bankers, both for advice and for implementation.

Investment banking in the United States began in the second half of the nineteenth century when a number of influential financiers helped the railroads and other huge industrial corporations get started. At that time, cash-rich Europeans looking for investments saw great opportunity for high returns in the burgeoning Americas. Investment bankers put the two together by helping their client corporations issue stocks and bonds that the bankers would sell to the Europeans. (By issuing bonds, a corporation is essentially writing an IOU, in which it agrees to pay all the money back to the bondholder, with interest. By issuing stock, a company is offering the investor partial ownership and the right to share in the firm's future profits.) This system supplied the emerging companies with money and the Europeans with investment opportunities.

The prestige and power of the investment banking community grew with the industrial giants of America, and as the decades passed close relationships were often formed between the two. One recent partner from Goldman Sachs was on the board of more than forty corporations during his career as an investment banker. Finding Wall Street luminaries on the board of directors of major corporations is still not uncommon today.

The accompanying chart shows the operations of a typical investment bank.

SERVICES TO CUSTOMERS

Investment bankers perform three basic services for their clients. First, they advise corporations on optimum financial and corporate strategies. Second, they put deals together, whether the deal involves offering new stock, floating long-term bonds, or issuing commercial paper.* Third, they distribute securities in the market through a number of means. Since different firms have different priorities, equal importance is not always placed on these three areas.

Corporate Finance

Corporate finance is the most traditional function of investment banks. In this capacity, firms advise corporations on different financing methods. For instance, if a company needs money to build a new plant, should it issue new stock or should it borrow short-term funds (less than one year) or long-term funds? Should the new money be acquired through public financing or private placement? The corporate finance adviser is expected to give the customer innovative ideas, the focus of which should be to save money for the corporation while providing it with the funds it needs for as long as it needs them. In order to do this effectively, the corporate financier must have an in-depth understanding of the company's business, its industry, and the financing vehicles that are available.

Municipal finance departments in investment banks provide the same services as corporate finance departments, only their clients are government entities, usually at the state, local,

THE MONEY JOBS INVESTMENT BANK

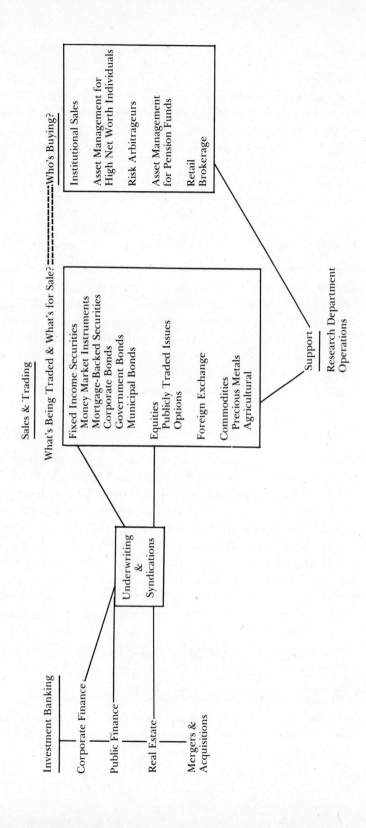

or municipal level. For instance, they might help New York State issue a bond to raise money for a hospital or school dormitory. Unlike corporate bonds, these issues are usually tax-free, which makes them very attractive to investors.

Until recently, a corporation's financing decisions were fairly simple. To raise short-term money, the corporation would issue commercial paper through an investment bank or else go to a commercial bank for a loan. For long-term money, the corporation would take the "plain vanilla" route: no-frills stocks or bonds, either placed privately with a group of investors or sold in the open market: With the volatile interest rates of the late 1970s and early 1980s, however, corporations became loath to pay the exorbitant expenses that might accompany new issues. As competition between the investment banks began to intensify, many were forced to come up with new products to satisfy both the issuing company and the investment community. The time had arrived for hybrid borrowing and investing vehicles with crazy names like TIGRS (TIGERS), CATS, double-dip leases, and adjustable-rate notes.

During this period, a particular product would come into vogue for perhaps two or three weeks, and deals would be pushed through the investment banking firms and into the market on very short notice. Timing was extremely important, because it was very difficult to predict where interest rates were going and thus to determine when the product would no longer make sense from the corporation's point of view. A number of firms became known for the products their wizards had invented and thus acquired reputations for certain specialties.

Traditionally, corporate finance departments in investment banks have been staffed by "generalists"—individuals who can advise on any financial product that might be appropriate for a corporation. The chief financial officer of a client firm would rely on the mystical wizards of Wall Street to know what was best for the company. Today things have changed. Because of the increasing importance of innovation and new products, many firms have now beefed up their corporate finance departments by adding a number of "specialists"—

people responsible for inventing and marketing products directly to the investment bank's client corporations. The theory is that the specialists can help firms to enhance their prestige and develop their own special place in the corporate community.

Today, most corporate treasury departments are highly sophisticated operations that rely on the investment bankers only for new ideas they might not have thought of themselves. Loyalty and historical (and sometimes even familial) ties have become less important. In addition, with the increasing competition posed to some of their operations by commercial banks, the investment banking firms have been forced to become more oriented toward business development and marketing. Ideas have increased in importance as family lineage has decreased.

Within the corporate finance department of an investment bank, the workload is usually divided among a number of client teams. Each team, consisting of two to four people, is responsible for developing and maintaining the firm's relationship with its client corporations, helping those clients evaluate the different financing methods available, preparing any necessary documentation—including prospectuses,* indenture agreements, and other documents required by law—and last, but definitely not least, determining the price at which a given security should be sold. This is a very important decision. If the price is too low, the corporate client may feel cheated; if the price is too high, the investment bank may be unable to market the security.

Underwriting and Syndications

If the corporate finance department has done its job, and if, after recommending a public offering, it has received a mandate from the client to handle a debt or equity issue, the underwriters are called in. When an investment bank underwrites a new stock offering, for instance, it buys the entire issue from the company, after which it is sold to other investors. Sometimes one firm will underwrite the entire offering, thus taking on the risk of selling it all to a finite client base. Usually, however, one firm will act as the originator (also called manager or lead) and will syndicate the deal by getting other investment banks to participate in the underwriting. Syndications are usually handled through a separate department within an investment house.* The originating firm, or manager, is responsible for organizing the syndicate, choosing the other firms to be included, and allotting blocks of shares to the participants. The syndicate can include as many as 70 different underwriters.

There are three common reasons for syndication. First, the originating firm may not be willing, or able, to accept the entire risk of reselling a securities issue and may choose to divide that risk among a number of firms. Second, syndication enlarges the distribution base for the secondary sale of a new issue. Many times, other firms are chosen for the syndicate because they are good at distributing securities—that is, they have a strong retail sales department and have many customers that they can tap for potential interest in the securities being offered. This is particularly true of "wire houses" like Merrill Lynch (so-called because all their branches are linked by extremely sophisticated communications equipment). Other times, members of a syndicate are chosen because they have a stronghold in geographic areas where many of the East Coast investment banks do not have a good market position. Finally, a customer may simply specify, for its own protection, that a syndicate be formed to spread their name throughout the financial marketplace or divvy up business to their favorite investment banks.

Sales and Trading

There are a number of ways underwriters can sell securities. Many times, they prefer selling large blocks of shares to institutional investor* clients. Institutional investors are pension funds, stock funds, and other large financial entities that own and trade huge amounts of securities. The investment banks can earn extravagant commissions in "block sales and trading" —selling large amounts of stock to their own client list as well as to outsiders. The institutional sales departments of investment banks are responsible for managing the relationships with institutional investors. Their goal is to handle as many securities transactions for their clients as possible, thus generating as much commission income for the firm as possible. Corporate finance departments increasingly consult sales personnel to determine if their institutional clients might be interested in purchasing a proposed new issue of debt or equity. This exchange of information can help the corporate finance department better service its own client base.

The trading operation in an investment bank deals in the secondary market (after the securities have been issued) for all types of financial instruments. These can be short-term T-Bills,* CDs, LIBOR* notes, or long-term bonds or stock. They trade for their own firm's account as well as for clients. Because they are constantly on top of new developments, traders are often in a position to advise the corporate finance department of opportunities—sometimes referred to as windows* on the market—that might arise for their clients. In fact, in some cases the trader may call a company directly to inform it of outstanding opportunities that may not exist in a matter of hours or days.

The sales and trading operations within an investment bank are closely intertwined. If the traders receive an order from a customer to sell, say 500,000 shares of a particular stock, the institutional salesforce hits the telephones and tries to help place the stock with its clients. In any transaction, the traders make money for the firm when they buy a security at a low price and sell it, either immediately or later on, at a higher price. This is called "buying low and selling high"—a familiar Wall Street chant.

In the old days, traders were considered second-class citizens compared with the corporate finance officers. At one investment bank, for instance, the corporate finance department was referred to as the "House of Lords," and the trading desk was called the "House of Commons." Today, however, this classification no longer exists. Good trading instincts are considered vital to the success of a corporate finance department. In fact, Morgan Stanley and First Boston recently switched management and now have traders as presidents!

BROKERAGE

E. F. Hutton, Dean Witter, and several other investment banks have retail brokerage operations, another means by which they can distribute securities in the market. Not all firms, however, have seen fit to engage in the so-called retail trade. A number of them, notably Morgan Stanley and First Boston, have targeted corporate clients and very high-net-worth customers only.

Brokers put buyers and sellers together for a commission. The higher the dollar amount of the transaction, the higher the commission. Therefore, a broker's aim is to get clients to buy or sell as often as possible. Historically, investors have traded more often in a rising or bull market, and price upswings are a broker's best friend.

Retail brokers are an investment bank's window to the general public. They act as go-betweens for individual investors and the initial underwriter. The most common type of broker is the stockbroker, who deals primarily in equities and bonds but has recently diversified into tax shelters and other areas. Stockbrokers advise clients on how to manage their assets, and often provide customers with research generated in the firm. This distinguishes them from discount brokers, who will only execute a trade and will not advise customers or provide them with any research materials. Because discount brokers provide fewer services, their commissions are lower, a feature that has made them attractive to some individual investors.

COMMODITIES

Some brokers trade financial instruments like stocks and bonds. Others trade commodities or staples, like soybeans, corn, and pork bellies. Traditionally, commodities brokers have operated independently of investment banks.

In recent years, however, two major mergers have occurred. In 1981 Goldman Sachs purchased J. Aron & Co., and in 1982 Phillip Brothers Commodities merged with Salomon Brothers, one of The Street's biggest players. These companies act as brokers for both institutional and retail (individual) investors, much as regular securities brokerage houses do. The only difference is that their primary products are commodities. (For a full explanation of the commodities market, see the industry reference books listed at the end of the book.)

Research

The research department of an investment bank supports the firm's sales and/or brokerage operations. Its main function is to provide reports on various companies and recommend either the purchase or sale of a company's stock on the basis of projected earnings. Analysts within the research department are responsible for keeping track of a particular industry—for example, the fast-food industry—and the companies within it. Analysts are really detectives. They must be able to look at numbers and spot trends before other people. But they must also be a little creative. Recently it was reported that an analyst went to a bar in a factory town to talk privately to factory workers about production problems inside a company he was following. This sort of information, which is usually not forthcoming in discussions with management, can be crucial to the performance of a company's stock. Analysts are expected to project which way a particular stock will move or how a particular company will do. They are considered successful if reality bears out their projections. Supposedly, the firm's institutional clients will benefit from this information by either buying or selling the stock of the company in question.

Analysts are constantly in contact with the top managers of the firms they are covering. These managers are, of course, quite anxious to make a good impression so that the analyst will release a "recommend" opinion on their stock, thus maximizing the stock's price in the secondary market. Reports generated by the research department are often used by sales and brokerage personnel to give advice to clients on how their own investments should be managed.

In recent years, some research analysts have begun to dabble in corporate finance as well. Because they have easy access to senior management at the companies they follow, analysts may be privy to information that is difficult for a corporate finance department to obtain. Because analysts spend so much time studying companies and their industries, they may be more aware of opportunities for the corporate finance department or even the mergers and acquisitions group. This growing relationship between the research and corporate finance areas has caused some consternation among the investment banks' corporate customers. They worry that information given to the investment bankers might be subject to the scrutiny of the analysts and thus adversely affect the price of their stock.

Investment banks also have analysts who are responsible for following and reporting on broad economic topics, such as the GNP and interest rate movements. An analyst who accurately predicts interest rate movements can be a great boon to a firm. Witness Henry Kaufman at Salomon Brothers, who for many years was considered the interest rate guru. If Henry Kaufman said interest rates were going to move, the market moved!

SPECIALTY AREAS

Some investment banks also have a number of specialty areas that do not fit neatly into any of the categories already mentioned. These operations include mergers and acquisitions, real estate, and asset management. Many firms have made their reputations in specialty areas. Lazard Frères, for instance, is known more than anything else for its expertise in mergers and acquisitions.

Mergers and Acquisitions

The most mysterious part of investment banking is, without a doubt, merger and acquisitions (M&A). In this arena, investment banks help companies plan the purchase or sale of another company or subsidiary. They also analyze potential acquisition targets and establish a fair price for them. In addition, they help companies fend off unfriendly takeovers. Recently, M&A has attracted a great deal of media attention, to a large extent because of the huge dollar amounts involved. For example, when Socal took over Gulf in 1984, the purchase price was over $12 billion. Handling a deal of this size is very attractive for the investment banks because of the generous

fees they can earn. Takeovers are cloaked in almost total se-
crecy so that potentially damaging rumors do not start flying
in the investment community. We know of one M&A specialist
who was severely reprimanded because he started discussing
a deal with his boss during a taxi ride uptown.

Real Estate

Another step in the diversification efforts of the investment
banks has been their move into corporate real estate. The real
estate group in an investment bank acts both as a principal,
and as an intermediary, by advising clients on potential strategies and tactics in the real estate market. As in the capital
markets, the primary responsibility of real estate is to put
investors and sellers (or sometimes developers) together. Investment banks with large retail brokerage operations, such as
Pru-Bache and Dean Witter, have recently placed a great deal
of emphasis on selling real estate tax shelters to their clients.

Asset Management

Investment banks also manage assets on behalf of institutions
and high-net-worth individuals. When corporations or unions
create pension funds, their responsibility is to invest the principal amount in such a way as to make it grow without subject-
ing the funds to unnecessary risks. The pension funds and
other institutions often spread their portfolio among a number of managers to defray the risks that any one individual
manager might take. These managers are akin to commercial
bank trust officers, but on a much larger scale. As a result,
people in asset management are usually drawn from other
areas within investment banks and are often senior members
of the firm. Corporations will often retain investment banks
or commercial bank trust departments, insurance company
pension departments, and small specialty or "boutique"
houses to handle their investments. Many of the smaller, independent companies have created substantial competitive
pressure in recent years because they have been able to get
better returns on their clients' portfolios than investment or
commercial banks.

Recently, both investment and commercial banks have begun to concentrate on the high-net-worth customer. The minimum investment in such an account is $100,000 to $250,000. In return for placing substantial assets with a firm, clients receive much the same services as institutional investors, including personalized investment advice from account executives who can help meet the individual's specific investment objectives. Most private banking departments are still relatively small, but they are growing rapidly.

JOB OPPORTUNITIES

Where are the jobs in investment banking? There are basically two tracks available: corporate finance and sales and trading. Either way, entry-level training in investment banks is quite different from that in commercial banks, because the emphasis is usually on the job rather than in the classroom.

Corporate Finance, Mergers and Acquisitions, and Real Estate

Most investment banks hire BAs in the corporate finance, mergers and acquisitions, and real estate divisions as two-year analysts. They work for only two years at the firm, after which time they are expected to go on to graduate school. Some of the investment banks, however, now ask their best analysts to stay on as associates, a role usually filled by newly hired MBAs. These associates are often encouraged to pursue their MBA at night, at the firm's expense.

Analysts are paid to number-crunch—that is, to perform ratio analyses, prepare projections, and evaluate strategies—as well as to carry out menial tasks, such as waiting at a printer's or lawyer's office until 2:00 or 3:00 A.M. for a prospectus or legal brief to be completed. This can cut into an analyst's personal life, but being involved in a major deal can make up for the late nights. It is important, however, to keep in mind that not all deals get done. Very often, junior people put in an incredible amount of time on a project that never comes to fruition. Learning to handle frustration is part of the training process.

135

Analysts usually work in a pool, where they are at the disposal of four or five associates and vice presidents. Their basic task is to supply their bosses with numerical analyses of a deal quickly and accurately. Analysts tend to work long and hard, putting in up to eighty hours over a typical six- or even seven-day week. The job is quite demanding, but the pay is usually very good. Moreover, two years spent at a major investment bank will certainly increase an analyst's chances of admission to one of the top business schools.

MBAs in these three areas are hired as associates. They have more responsibility and less "gruntwork" than the analysts, but they are in the office just as late at night. MBAs are hired as the equivalent of new associates at a law firm. Because many of the investment banks are still privately held, partnerships* are aggressively pursued. Partners have a direct share in the profits of the firm and a major role in its management. The jobs are very demanding, but an MBA with the right kind of work experience can start at $45,000 to $60,000, plus bonuses.

Sales and Trading

As the name implies, sales and trading training programs are designed to prepare both BAs and MBAs for positions in sales and trading. Generally speaking, training consists of a number of rotational assignments followed by permanent placement. In addition, salespeople and traders must take the Series Seven* exam to become registered reps* (representatives). The firm will usually help them prepare for this by subsidizing their attendance at the New York Institute of Finance, a local organization, or by putting them through an in-house program. Initially, trainees always serve as backups, merely observing how things are done and perhaps running out to get coffee for the traders.

The atmosphere of a trading room is worlds apart from that of a corporate finance department. Tension and often hysteria reign at the trading desk, where split-second decisions can result in profits or losses of literally millions of dollars.

The background of a typical trader has changed significantly in recent years. In the old days, it was not unheard of

THE DAY OF A CORPORATE ANALYST
IN A WALL STREET INVESTMENT BANK

THREE WHAT-IF SCENARIOS [a]
by Kevin Callaghan

	Scenario I *Piece-of-Cake Day*	Scenario II *Run-of-the-Mill Day*	Scenario III *Balls-of-Fire Day*
Percentage of Career in this Mode	10% [b]	70%	20%
Arrival Time	9:30 A.M.	9:00 A.M.	8:15 A.M.
Previous Night's Sleep	5½ hours [c]	7 hours	4 hours
Workplace	"friendly, fun environment"	"the bullpen"	"a real hell hole"
Daily Activities			
Work with annual reports	0.5 hours [d]	2.5 hours	5 hours
Calculator and personal computer spread-sheeting	0.5	3.0	5.0
Writing: text and letters	0.5	1.5	2.0
Talking on phone with friends	1.0	.25	not applicable
Proofreading/ xeroxing/ collating	0.25	1.0	2.0
Meeting with senior members of project team	0.75 [e]	1.0	1.25

	Scenario I *Piece-of-Cake Day*	Scenario II *Run-of-the-Mill Day*	Scenario III *Balls-of-Fire Day*
Lunch:			
Place	South Street Seaport	cafeteria	not applicable
Time	1.5 hours	0.5–0.75 hours	not applicable
Client contact (conference calls or meetings)	0.5 [f]	0.75 [f]	0.25 [f]
Reading business publications and research reports, and checking stocks on Quotron	1.5	0.5–0.75	0.25
Talking with other analysts	1.0	0.75	0.25
TOTAL	8.0 hours	12 hours	16 hours [g]

WEIGHTED AVERAGE LENGTH OF ANALYST'S DAY: 12.4 hours

[a] A fourth, all too possible, scenario, the "Weekend at the Office," is not treated here.

[b] Increases to 30% for second-year analysts in their last two months of work and to 50% for those second-year analysts with acceptances to Harvard and/or Stanford Business School.

[c] Two reasons: (1) previous day was also a piece-of-cake day with evening spent at bars with commercial banker friends; or (2) previous day was balls-of-fire day to finish presentation in time for vice president to take to morning meeting.

[d] Reviewing potential personal investments.

[e] Just when you thought you were free for the weekend, the call comes at 4:30 P.M. "Are you very busy? Why don't you stop by and see me?" Translation: "You're mine for the weekend."

[f] Daily average for the month.

[g] This is not to be construed as an upper limit.

to hire traders without college degrees. Now, most newcomers have MBAs or are BAs with significant work experience. Ultimately, a good trader must have market savvy, excellent concentration, and an ability to make quick decisions under pressure. One trader ranks his peers according to their ability to forget the original purchase price of a particular security. Good traders price solely by the current market. Losses, after all, are part of the game. It is not inconceivable for a senior trader to lose $25,000 on Monday, double that on Tuesday, and make it all back on Wednesday.

TYPICAL DAY IN THE LIFE OF A TRADER †

7:30 A.M.	Arrive at office. Read *The Wall Street Journal* and *The New York Times*. Read firm's economists' opinions on yesterday's market activities and what is expected from the Fed. (Two trainees are responsible for distributing technical analysis to traders.)
8:00–8:15 A.M.	Find out what the firm did overseas the night before.
8:30 A.M.	"Sit in" on morning meeting via speaker phone to all branch offices. Head trader gives opinion of market; economists give summation of what happened the day before.
8:45 A.M.	Find out what early call is in bond futures pit.
9:00 A.M.	Market opens; buy low and sell high.
11:40 A.M.	Fed time. See whether the Fed is going to be in the market.
12:30 P.M.	Lunch (at desk). Rarely if ever go out.
5:00–5:30 P.M.	Market closes; check closing position.
	Go to Harry's Bar on Hanover Square for drinks on the brokers.

† Courtesy of a junior trader at a major New York securities firm.

Traders who do well for the firm are rewarded, and well. Rumor has it that one trader at a major investment bank was given a bonus of over $1 million for his performance. He went to see the firm's partners and told them it wasn't a big enough bonus, that he wanted twice that much. When they turned him down, he took the $1 million and walked, retiring at the ripe old age of 30-something. Not all traders make seven figures, but traders do live well if they're good. If they're not good, they won't be traders for very long!

If you look around a trading room, you'll notice that few traders are over the age of 35 (although some might look 100). The intense pressure of the trading room takes its toll, and many traders over 30 go into sales or some other area of the firm. Put it this way, if you like to go out to lunch, forget a career in trading.

Sales is also a fast-paced area, although not quite as intense as trading. Salespeople are not committing the firm's money the way traders are, but they must constantly be in touch with the institutional investors to advise them on different trades over the course of the day. Depending on the house, salespeople are paid either a base salary plus bonus or strictly a commission. A good sales representative with a few years of experience should earn a minimum of $100,000.

Brokers are a variation on the sales rep theme. Retail brokerage training programs are designed to give trainees the technical background necessary to pass the registered representative exam administered by the SEC. Brokers are also taught marketing and sales methods to help them generate more business. After all, in the final analysis, brokers are salespeople. After training, brokers are given business cards, a desk, and a telephone. It is then up to them to generate business and thereby commissions for themselves as they are being weaned from their salary. Since brokers are selling to the general investing public, age is a factor in the hiring process. Clients find it reassuring to entrust their life savings to a broker they regard as mature. Work experience or an MBA is a prerequisite at most investment houses. Many will not hire brokers under the age of 26.

It takes a certain personality type to be a successful broker.

When a trainee starts out, he or she has to deal with rejection day in and day out—people may hang up the telephone or just not express any interest. The successful broker must have an optimistic attitude about the prospects of each and every phone call before even picking up the receiver. A positive, professional attitude is, in the end, what will land the business. Recruiters, therefore, look for strong selling skills and a professional demeanor.

As a rule, investment banking firms pay the highest starting salaries, for both BAs and MBAs in the financial services industry. They pay well because they want to attract the best talent available. One Wall Streeter told us that an investment banker really only needs three things: common sense, diligence, and endurance. Of course, intelligence, work experience, and an Ivy League degree don't hurt! Depending on the individual firm, investment banks demand workweeks of 55 to 80 hours. It is a standard joke that, before bonuses, analysts and associates at investment banks barely make the minimum hourly wage. Working until 8:00 or 9:00 every night is not uncommon, even for partners. Since many investment banks are partnerships, the shareholders' long hours are for their own benefit. Partnership also encourages investment banking houses to hire fewer people than they might otherwise, since the firm's expense is the partners' expense.

In return for long hours and high pressure, employees receive a number of perquisites. They are usually remunerated for taxis and dinner if they work late. Entertaining clients is commonplace, so tickets to theater and sporting events can sometimes appear out of the blue. And, if the firm does well, employees will probably receive a bonus. Since investment banks have performed well in recent years, many employees take a large annual bonus for granted. Unless a bonus is specifically guaranteed, however, it cannot be relied on. Finally, bonuses also reflect the firm's opinion of an employee's productivity—star performers are usually compensated accordingly.

The investment banking community is more difficult to penetrate than commercial banking, insurance, or accounting. Contacts within a firm, therefore, are extremely valuable. By the same token, once inside, an employee will always have access to the mysteries of The Street. If demand for jobs is any indication, investment banks will continue to attract some of the brightest, most talented individuals entering the business world.

J. C. Bradford & Co.
170 4th Avenue North
Nashville, Tennessee 37219
(615) 748-9000

J. C. Bradford & Co. is a regional securities company that bills itself as the "Southeast's largest investment banking firm." It is a relatively small operation and thus offers a more personal working environment than might be found in one of the New York-based wire houses.

Each year, Bradford hires 70 to 80 broker trainees. They begin with a three-month programmed self-instruction course designed to prepare them for the Series Seven exam. During this time, trainees also develop prospect lists of 2,000 to 3,000 names, to be used once they start working. After this, they undergo a two-week training course on such topics as product knowledge, product suitability, selling skills, and telephone prospecting. Much of the training relies on simulation and role-playing methods. Trainees are given the opportunity to make fools of themselves before they go out and face customers. After these classes, trainees go out in the field and spend five months prospecting for customers. Then they return to training to correct any bad habits they may have picked up.

Bradford also runs a training program for employees who have been working in the office in lower-level jobs. Around 45 to 50 candidates are nominated each year by their supervisors to participate in the program, which is designed to give trainees a strong working knowledge of the securities business and how it is conducted at Bradford. Homework assignments and exams are given. In some cases, it is possible to move from a support position to a brokerage job.

Starting salaries at Bradford are a function of the individual's background—both BAs and MBAs with all kinds of work

142

experience are hired. The company likes to see candidates with fairly developed selling skills. Broker trainees are started off on a training salary, but after passing the Series Seven exam they get a base salary plus commissions. Benefits include Blue Cross/Blue Shield, life insurance, retirement plan, tuition reimbursement, and reduced commissions on stock transactions.

Brown Brothers Harriman & Co.
59 Wall Street
New York, New York 10005
(212) 483-1818

Brown Brothers is the oldest and largest privately owned investment bank in the United States, with a very "upper crust" client base. Because of certain grandfather clauses in banking law, the firm is permitted to have commercial banking offices in more than one state. It is very strong internationally in managing U.S. investments for foreigners. It also manages brokerage accounts for high-net-worth individuals in a very conservative fashion. The firm is divided into two major divisions: banking, which includes lending, corbanking, foreign exchange trading, and bond and money market trading, and investment, which includes sales, brokerage, and research.

In recent years Brown Brothers has hired between ten and fifteen BAs and five to seven MBAs annually. Of this amount, two-thirds have gone into the banking division, with the remainder going into the investment division. This is a very difficult bank to penetrate, so connections really help. Training is primarily on the job and is designed to introduce new hires to all aspects of the bank. Both bankers and investors go through a six-month rotational period before their first full-time, one-year assignment. For approximately two months during this period, bankers and investors rotate through each other's divisions. This experience gives them the opportunity to meet people in other areas of the organization whom they can call on for help and advice later in their careers.

After the rotations, bankers are given a one-year assignment in foreign exchange, bonds, money markets, or cor-banking. Investment trainees go into international banking, investment advisory services (including research), institutional asset management, personal services, bonds or equity trading. Trainees indicate that the firm takes individual preferences into account for this one-year assignment. During this time, they also attend afternoon classes with trainees from Bank of New York. Courses in accounting and financial analysis skills are held two or three afternoons per week.

Brown Brothers did not provide us with salary information, but the trainees we spoke with indicated that BAs start at $23,000 but make $24,500 within six months. Benefits include major medical and dental coverage, life insurance, reduced commissions on stock transactions, and tuition reimbursement.

First Boston Corporation
Park Avenue Plaza
New York, New York 10055
(212) 909-2000

First Boston was founded in 1934 as a public firm. Traditionally known for its strength in corporate finance, and M&A in particular, First Boston has expanded its scope in recent years. In 1978, for example, First Boston and Crédit Suisse developed an international partnership, Financière Crédit Suisse–First Boston, with an emphasis on international merchant banking. First Boston owns 31 percent of the partnership, which in turn owns 29 percent of First Boston, CSFB, as it is commonly known, is the Euromarket* leader in both bond and floating-rate note issues. In 1982, First Boston Real Estate and Development Corporation was founded, giving the firm access to additional markets.

First Boston had one of the first analyst programs on The Street: a structured eight-week in-house program that hires a diverse cross-section of analysts. The formal program which began with 9 analysts in 1978, has grown to an estimated 75 in 1984 (numbers include both first- and second-year analysts). Analysts now account for over 20 percent of the professionals in the corporate and public finance departments. The program continues to expand, with hiring projected to increase to over 40 in 1984. Competition for these spots is fierce. Over 2,000 résumés are submitted annually, with a heavy concentration coming from Ivy League graduates.

First Boston looks at qualified applicants throughout the year, so if you graduate in January, or are interested in starting sometime other than the summer, send in your résumé. Approximately 80 percent of the analysts are hired for corporate finance, with the balance starting in public finance. This is a two-year program, but the firm does allow analysts to stay somewhat longer before they move on to business school. Although statistics are somewhat meager thus far, it is interesting to note that all former First Boston analysts who returned to Wall Street after graduate school accepted offers to join the firm.

FB's analyst program is probably more organized than those at the other New York investment banks. It includes a structured eight-week program, and during this time participants are relieved of all office duties. They begin with an intensive six-week class in accounting and corporate finance taught by a former professor from the Columbia Graduate School of Business. Classes are held at the Williams Club in Manhattan starting in July, and both midterms and final exams are given. The courses rely on case studies supplemented by text, and long hours of nightly preparation are required of most participants.

The second phase of training is orientation to the firm. Over a two-week period, senior management makes presentations on the departments comprising First Boston. This gives analysts a better understanding of how the firm operates in general, as well as a better idea of what careers might interest them in particular. During the course of their two-year stay at First Boston, analysts receive additional training through seminars, which are usually scheduled for one night a week. The firm also feels that investment banking is an "experience" business and that the best way to learn is to be involved in actual deals as they are being conceptualized, proposed, and executed. Thus analysts are given plenty of opportunities for on-the-job activities.

MBA associates are hired in sales and trading as well as in

the corporate finance department. Total hiring ranges from fifteen to twenty MBAs per year. Since associates who join the firm generally have a stronger financial background than analysts, their training program consists of the two-week orientation, study classes for the registered representative exam, and a series of rotations. Finance associates go through two weeks of rotations, while salespeople and traders rotate for a few months.

Salaries begin at approximately $24,000 for BAs and $40,000-plus for MBAs. Because associates do not have the lure of future partnership (the firm is public), First Boston usually offers big salaries and big bonuses. Bonuses, however, vary widely and are based "solely on merit." Benefits include major medical and dental coverage, life insurance, and reduced commissions on stock transactions.

First Jersey Securities
50 Broadway
New York, New York 10004
(212) 269-5500

First Jersey is an extremely aggressive privately owned investment banking and brokerage firm that has been in existence for ten years. At present, First Jersey has 23 offices scattered across the United States, but that number is sure to grow, as are the requirements for entry-level hires.

First Jersey offers account executive positions to BAs and MBAs. According to its recruiting literature, these opportunities come with *"very big money potential"* (the firm's emphasis). First Jersey told us that their hiring in a given year is directly related to market activity. Account executives work on a straight commission basis as stockbrokers. As such, they seek to build their client list, service portfolios, and keep customers abreast of market fluctuations on a regular basis.

Before becoming account executives, new hires must take outside training to pass the Series Seven exam. Interestingly enough, trainees at First Jersey are responsible for paying the cost of the exam and all materials, which may run to $300.

Salaries are straight commission. Benefit information was unavailable.

Goldman Sachs
85 Broad Street
New York, New York 10004
(212) 902-1000

Goldman Sachs is perhaps the most prestigious of the special bracket* investment houses. In 1983 the firm was ranked number one in industry studies for serving corporations and banks. Goldman, which has remained a private firm, has an excellent reputation in just about everything it does, and this makes it one of the most difficult places in the world to get a job. For example, every year the firm gets applications from 1,500 MBAs for 30 positions and from 2,500 BAs for 20 to 25 jobs.

In 1976, Goldman began an analyst program that currently accepts from 20 to 25 BAs with diverse backgrounds—from economics majors to art history majors, Analysts are hired by specific divisions, including corporate finance, mergers and acquisitions, real estate, international corporate finance, utilities, mortgage-backed securities, capital markets, private finance, leveraged buyouts, and municipal finance.

The analyst program begins each September, with classroom sessions lasting three to four hours per day over two to three weeks. Classes are taught by business school professors from New York University and cover financial accounting and statement analysis. A series of in-house seminars is initiated during this period and continues intermittently after the formal program is completed. Analysts usually stay with Goldman from 18 to 24 months, after which time they move on to business school.

Goldman also has a securities and sales training program that accepts 12 to 25 people per year, mostly MBAs. Salespeople and traders may be assigned to New York headquarters or to a regional location, although all training is done in New York. Most of the training period, which lasts about a year, is spent on the job. From 8:30 to 5:00, new hires sit next to experienced traders and salespeople and go through a series of rotations. The program uses interactive videotapes to simulate work situations and suggest solutions. Selling skills

147

are also emphasized, and are taught through video sessions, case studies, and cold-call simulations in which associates call experienced salespeople at other offices who pretend to be customers. Seminars are held for six weeks on such topics as equities, fixed-income securities, investment banking, investment research, operations, international, and trading and arbitrage.*

Training for the registered representative exam is provided through a course given at the New York Institute of Finance. In addition, trainees spend some time in operations, familiarizing themselves with the nuts and bolts of million-dollar transactions. All Goldman trainees have a "big buddy," a senior sales representative or trader designated to help out new hires whenever possible. A somewhat similar training program is offered in Goldman's J. Aron Division, a precious metals trading operation that the firm purchased in 1981.

Salaries at Goldman vary from unit to unit because each area does its own hiring. Generally, BAs begin at $25,000-plus; Goldman told us officially that MBAs begin at approximately $45,000. Other sources within the firm have told us of MBAs who started as high as $70,000. Bonuses are usually granted as well. Benefits include major medical and dental coverage, life insurance, reduced commissions on stock transactions, free checking from Citibank, and tuition reimbursement.

Hambrecht & Quist Incorporated
235 Montgomery Street
San Francisco, California 94104
(415) 433-1720

Hambrecht & Quist is an investment bank and venture capital firm that specializes in technology-based companies. The firm is a major player in the initial public offerings market. In addition to its San Francisco headquarters, the firm maintains offices in New York, Boston, London, Menlo Park, and Los Angeles.

Each year, H&Q hires a number of MBAs to join its MBA management training program, which is designed to provide new hires with an understanding of the firm in general and how the various departments interact. Training consists of rotations through various departments, including corporate finance, venture capital, research, and sales and trading. Each rotation lasts a minimum of two months, and trainees work closely with senior staff members. After six months with the firm, a trainee becomes eligible for permanent placement. The maximum training period is one year. The rotational system gives trainees the opportunity to decide where they might like to work; it also gives Hambrecht & Quist the opportunity to evaluate trainees. In addition to the rotations, trainees attend weekly and monthly meetings and seminars conducted by managing directors and associates of the firm.

H&Q also hires four to six MBAs who do not wish to go through such a long rotational period and who are more sure of where their interest lies. These candidates are hired primarily into corporate finance, venture capital, research, and sales and trading. They undergo a training period of two to three months, during which time they rotate through these departments. These new hires also attend the weekly and monthly seminars with the other trainees.

Salaries begin at $40,000 and bonuses are awarded on the basis of performance. The company would not disclose benefit information.

E. F. Hutton & Co.
One Battery Park Plaza
New York, New York 10004
(212) 742-5000

E. F. Hutton, the second-largest securities firm in the country in terms of number of registered representatives, is also an important investment bank (one of the ten largest underwriters in 1982). Hutton's investment banking operations are relatively new, having been established eighteen years ago. Corporate finance activities are performed in New York as well as through offices in Charlotte (North Carolina), Chicago, Houston, Los Angeles, San Francisco, and Paris.

Hutton hires BAs and MBAs into its sixteen-week account

149

executive* training program, which includes on-the-job training and formal coursework. The classes are designed to train individuals for the Series Seven exam. At first, trainees receive orientation to the branch where they will eventually be placed. At the same time, they prepare for the registered representative exam. After they become registered, trainees spend two weeks at Hutton's training facilities in New York. Here, they attend classes from 8:30 A.M. to 5:30 P.M., Monday to Friday, on a wide array of topics, including fixed-income securities, options, annuities, municipal bonds, and underwritings. After this, they return to the original branch and are instructed in salesmanship and prospecting techniques.

Hutton also has an accelerated management training program for MBAs who want to become branch office managers or product managers in the brokerage operation. Individuals are hired annually for this three-year program. In the first year, participants receive account executive training and work in the branch office. In the second year, participants are given assistant manager training and continue to work in the branch. In the third year, they go through management training while still working in the branch. The program requires a number of relocations, and the firm likes to see MBAs with one to three years of sales experience.

On the investment banking side, Hutton hires BAs as two-year analysts and MBAs as associates each year. Unlike other investment banks, Hutton does not have its analysts report to associates. Rather they report directly to vice presidents and assistant vice presidents; and from what we've heard they are responsible for performing the same level of work as their MBA counterparts. There is not much in the way of structured training for BAs. The firm holds a three-week accounting course attended by analysts and associates. Classes are held for three to four hours each morning, and according to our sources, homework assignments can take three to four hours each night to prepare. To add to the time pressure, associates and analysts work on deals while participating in classroom training. Tests are administered throughout the course. Subsequently, classes on special accounting topics are held on Friday evenings or Saturday mornings and last two to three hours each.

Associates are hired to be generalists, at least for one year. Following exposure to the investment banking department as a whole, associates may be assigned to an industry group, such as energy, telecommunications, or transportation. They may also be hired into the public finance department. In this case, associates rotate through municipal trading, syndications, and research. At the same time, they are given computer training to gain familiarity with the technology used.

Hutton would not disclose salary information. BA analysts we spoke with reported starting salaries of $24,000 plus bonuses. Benefits for staff members include life and health insurance and stock purchase opportunities.

Kidder Peabody & Co.
10 Hanover Square
New York, New York 10005
(212) 747-2000

Kidder Peabody is a relatively large, privately held investment bank with 73 offices and 5,200 employees around the globe. It provides the full range of investment banking services. Kidder's strengths lie primarily in corporate finance and investment research. It is among the six largest investment banks in terms of number of corporate finance professionals. Kidder is also expanding its sales and trading area.

There is very little structured training at Kidder. The firm hires ten to fifteen BAs per year for a two-year analyst program. Analysts go into either corporate finance or public finance. The firm also hires ten to fifteen MBAs to serve as generalists in the corporate finance department for two years before moving into such specialty groups as M&A, private placements, bank and financial services, energy, technology, project and lease finance, Kidder Peabody Realty, and new business development.

Both BAs and MBAs attend two weeks of orientation sessions when they join the firm. Classes are provided in specialized topics, such as underwriting, financial futures, and rating agencies. Trainees are then assigned to account teams and serve as backups, providing analytical support to their seniors.

BAs start at around $23,500, with MBAs starting at over

$40,000. Benefits include major medical and dental coverage, life insurance, profit sharing (bonus), reduced commissions on stock transactions, and store and theater discounts.

Lehman Brothers Kuhn Loeb
55 Water Street
New York, New York 10041
(212) 558-1500

Lehman has recently been purchased by Shearson/AMEX. We have kept the listings separate because it is still uncertain whether they will continue to run autonomously. Founded in 1850, the firm had approximately 80 partners and 3,000 employees, having tripled in size over the last ten years.

The fastest growth area within the firm was in the distribution (sales and trading) segment, which represents two-thirds of the professional employees in the firm. This large distribution network is one of Lehman's major strengths. Apart from institutional sales and block trading, Lehman also has a retail network of high-net-worth individuals. In addition, the firm manages over $10 billion through the various funds it administers. Lehman's research department also enjoys a good reputation on The Street.

On the banking side, Lehman is known primarily for its M&A work. The firm handles many deals under $50 million but also gets involved in some of the biggest mergers on Wall Street. Lehman is the only house with a specialized divestitures group, and it was the first to form a financial restructuring group. Overall, Lehman likes to think of itself as striking a good balance among its three operating groups: distribution, banking, and asset management.

Competition for job openings at Lehman is very high. One employee remarked that the firm was interested in only 200 of the 60,000 MBAs graduating annually in the United States —the same ones all the major investment banks court. As far as the opportunities for BAs are concerned, Lehman's analyst program is one of the newer ones in town, but it has matured quickly in terms of size and the exposure offered participants. There are currently over 60 analysts at Lehman, and hiring will likely continue at the rate of 25 to 30 per year. Of those hired, approximately 20 percent will be in public finance. Before their on-the-job assignments begin, analysts go through a six-week formalized program whose primary function is to "socialize" new hires into the firm and give them the basic tools needed to handle their initial assignments.

The core of the program is a three-week accounting course taught by an outside professor. Further training is provided in corporate finance and in the use of personal computers, an analyst's best friend. An exam is given at the end of the accounting course but is not used for evaluation.

Analysts and associates attend a series of orientation seminars together. As at other firms, senior management and specialists from various areas make presentations on how their units function and how they fit into the firm's structure and strategic plans. After this portion of training, analysts are assigned into a bullpen as generalists or into a specific area on a temporary basis. In keeping with its overall philosophy that a good investment banker must have varied experiences, the firm rotates analysts two or three times during their two-year stay. A few top analysts are invited to continue with the firm as associates after two years, but usually only a handful remain.

Associates at Lehman are exposed to all facets of the business at an early stage in their careers. Even banking associates take the registered representative exam to better familiarize themselves with the firm's range of products and services. The associate program has three elements: in-house lectures and orientation, rotations, and courses held at the New York Institute of Finance. Rotations are particularly important for those hired into the distribution side of the business. The entire sales and trading program lasts sixteen weeks and is one of the few on The Street to include non-MBAs. Sitting with sales reps and traders gives associates a good feel for the departments they will be working in and a chance to observe seasoned professionals in action. As in other areas, associates in sales and trading are given the opportunity for movement within the firm after two years.

Analysts start at salaries in the mid-twenties plus bonus and are given three weeks of vacation. Associates in finance start at approximately $40,000 plus bonus and receive four weeks of vacation. Benefits include major medical and dental coverage, life insurance, reduced commissions on stock transactions, discounts on credit cards, and relocation expenses if applicable.

Merrill Lynch & Co.
One Liberty Plaza
New York, New York 10080
(212) 637-7455

Merrill Lynch is one of the largest diversified financial services companies in the world, providing investment banking, retail brokerage, insurance, and real estate services to more than 4 million clients the world over. Merrill is the largest securities firm in the country in terms of equity, employs the largest number of registered representatives, and has the largest corporate finance staff. As a publicly held firm, the company is not quite as flexible as some of the smaller houses. But in many respects it offers the best training available for those interested in a financial services career.

Merrill's unrivaled retail base makes its operations area absolutely essential to the firm's profitability. The firm, therefore, has developed programs expressly for the operations area, the largest employer in the company. These programs are designed to train managers for both the home office and the branch network. An operations manager's function is to ensure that the work of maintaining accounts flows smoothly and that any mistakes that do occur are quickly corrected. These positions consist primarily of managing back room and clerical staffs. Strong interpersonal and organizational skills are a must.

Merrill Lynch runs two programs to train operations managers: an operations interns development program and an accelerated operations management program. They last eighteen and twelve months respectively and have from 10 to 14 participants each. On-the-job training makes up 60 percent of each program. In-house courses are given in specific areas, such as accounting and reporting procedures. Participants are put on the line quickly so that they can see various units in action. When the need arises, trainees are moved to specific areas to act as troubleshooters. Those involved in the accelerated operations training program are slated to work in one of the offices outside New York. Thus geographic mobility is an absolute requirement.

Merrill Lynch has a vast hardware network linking all of its accounts, and each year its corporate systems program trains 40 to 50 people to run it. The program is divided into two segments: business applications and systems programming. The business applications program consists of three months of classwork followed by on-the-job training. No specific major is required, but some experience with COBOL and AS-SEMBLER languages is helpful. The classwork is very rigorous, and trainees are required to write ten programs. Training is highly quantitative and demands strong analytical skills. After completion of the courses, trainees go directly into one of the 25 areas where they are needed.

The systems programming class lasts fifteen weeks and is designed to prepare computer science majors with a working knowledge of JCL and ASSEMBLER for positions as systems architects and managers. Systems architects work on integrating the different programs so that they all work together. After training on Merrill Lynch systems, each trainee is given his or her own terminal to use for the duration of training.

The most competitive program at Merrill is the corporate internship, which lasts 18 to 24 months. In 1983, for example, 2,000 applications were submitted, 800 applicants were interviewed, 100 were called back, and 18 received offers. The program is extremely popular because of the excellent exposure it gives interns to the firm as a whole. Interestingly, this broad exposure has also been cited as the program's only shortcoming, because the relatively short rotations do not afford interns the opportunity to get deeply involved in a specific area.

The program begins with a week-long orientation followed by a nine-week stint at a retail sales office. Interns also take the account executive training program, which is taught at the

Donald T. Regan School, Merrill's New York training center. This is a very formal program designed to give candidates sufficient background to pass the registered representative exam. Interns spend another four weeks in product school, learning the range of products and services that Merrill offers.

After the stint in retail sales, interns rotate through various areas of the firm under individually tailored programs. Typically, interns spend time in securities research, marketing services, sales, capital markets, and real estate. Each rotation lasts six to eight weeks. After their first year in the program, corporate interns are encouraged to attend New York University Business School at night, at Merrill's expense. After the program is completed, interns may choose virtually any area of the firm for permanent placement.

Merrill Lynch's capital markets division also offers traditional two-year analysts positions for approximately fifteen to twenty BAs per year. There are four weeks of formal training, with seminars in accounting, the securities industry, and Merrill Lynch systems. Analysts either are assigned to a specific group or operate as generalists during the first year. They are then given the option of switching assignments for their second year.

The firm also hires approximately fifteen MBAs per year as associates in corporate finance, and fifteen in sales and trading. Both groups of MBAs go through an orientation seminar and take the account executive training course for the registered representative exam. After this, the trainees are rotated for approximately twelve weeks and are then sent out to one of the twelve regional offices for six weeks to gain a broader perspective on the firm.

Salaries start in the low to mid-twenties for BAs and mid-thirties for MBAs. Bonuses are awarded to revenue producers. Benefits include major medical and dental coverage, life insurance, pension plan, reduced commissions on stock transactions, and tuition reimbursement.

Morgan Stanley & Co.
1251 Avenue of the Americas
New York, New York 10020
(212) 974-4000

Morgan Stanley, one of the special bracket investment banks, is probably the most tradition-bound house on The Street. Spun off from the Morgan bank after the passage of Glass-Steagall in 1933, Morgan Stanley is still known as the "white shoe" firm because of its partners' Ivy League backgrounds. Morgan Stanley, however, has recently made an effort to change its public image. It has moved from dealing exclusively with blue chip firms to competing on a more direct basis with the other Wall Street houses. For example, the firm now handles one of the Teamsters' pension funds. Also, the sales and trading area has gained prestige recently with a number of people from this side serving as managing directors.

Morgan Stanley trains entry-level employees almost entirely on the job. BAs are hired almost exclusively as analysts with the expectation that they will return to school after two years. Analysts are hired primarily into the investment banking group, which consists of corporate finance, investment banking services, mergers and acquisitions, and international operations. Investment banking services is Morgan Stanley's marketing arm for domestic clients whom it refers to the three functional areas: investment banking, real estate, and sales and trading. Capital markets, or sales and trading, hires only MBAs.

Morgan Stanley hires from 35 to 45 analysts per year. Competition for these spots is very keen because of the training and exposure to senior management offered. On-the-job responsibilities, which start immediately upon joining the firm, consist of providing much of the backup for associates and managing directors in packaging deals.

The firm rehires approximately 25 percent of former Morgan Stanley analysts after they complete graduate school.

All MBAs are hired at the associate level in one of four areas: investment banking, financial planning and analysis, capital markets, and real estate. The investment banking

157

group hires almost half the MBAs taken on by the firm in any given year. Virtually all associates in investment banking start in corporate finance or mergers and acquisitions, where they are trained in the entire process of packaging a financial deal: analysis, presentation, and execution. Generally, associates achieve a certain amount of mobility within the organization only after completing extensive work in a particular department. Associates, like analysts, work on teams and are often involved with two or three deals at once. In Morgan Stanley's words, "The firm places a premium on an associate's ability to assume the responsibility for as much of the workload as possible."

The financial planning and analysis (FP&A) group is viewed as an internal consulting unit that analyzes developments within the firm as well as in the marketplace. Because of this broad function, those hired into FP&A receive a thorough introduction to Morgan Stanley's individual areas. Responsibilities range from strategic and tactical investment planning to general economic analysis. Presentations are prepared by teams, with analysts compiling data for the associates, who concentrate it and present the conclusions to managing directors.

The capital markets group—comprising research, syndications, equity and fixed-income trading and sales, money market activities, and asset management—has been expanded at Morgan Stanley in recent years. Approximately twelve MBAs are hired into this area annually. Associates are not hired to fill a specific spot (trading mortgage-backed securities, for instance). Rather, they rotate through the various line areas, where they sit with traders and salespeople to learn about specific products and services that the firm offers and that they might be interested in. Individual rotations last from two to three weeks, during which time participants are given reference materials to help them prepare for the registered representative exam. After completing their rotations, associates are assigned to specific desks. They are given some opportunity to express their preference, but generally they are placed where the firm needs them most.

Morgan Stanley has two separate real estate subsidiaries:

Brooks Harvey, which specializes in real estate projects, and Morstan Incorporated, which advises clients and invests on the firm's behalf. Responsibilities include analyzing market conditions and structuring specific proposals for presentation to prospective and existing clients.

Each year Morgan Stanley offers a unique management information systems (MIS) program to six groups of approximately nine qualified candidates. One of the guidelines for consideration for the program is a combined 1400 on the SATs. An extensive background in computers is not essential. This is a highly competitive program in which performers are very well compensated and nonperformers are asked to leave.

During the twelve-month MIS program, participants spend about a quarter of their time in class. Seminars include statistics (one semester's equivalent is taught in six weeks, with one or two class sessions per week), investment banking (one week) and preparation for the registered representative exam (fifteen weeks for ten hours per week). In addition to in-class responsibilities, participants spend at least 40 hours a week working with the firm's electronic data processing systems. Successful MIS employees write programs for the firm's operational needs or for specific applications, such as trading for Morgan Stanley's account on the basis of computer analyses of particular issues.

Analysts start at a minimum of $24,000 plus bonus. Starting salaries in the MIS program are $26,200. Associates are reported to start at a minimum of $40,000 plus bonus. Benefits include major medical and dental coverage, life insurance, profit sharing, pension plan, and reduced commissions on stock transactions.

The O'Conner Partnerships
141 West Jackson Boulevard
Suite 3140
Chicago, Illinois 60604
(312) 322-9525

The O'Conner Partnerships was founded in 1977 as a stock option trading company. Starting in Chicago, home of the

Chicago Board of Trade and the Chicago Board of Options Exchange, with fewer than 10 employees, the firm now has over 150. It trades on virtually all the financial exchanges in the United States, working mainly in financial futures and options. As the firm continues to grow, opportunities will become available in a number of other areas, including trading, economics, mathematics, portfolio management, securities analysis, and computer science. At present, the majority of their recruiting is for trading positions.

New hires spend two or three months on the job before beginning with a one-month structured program consisting of taped presentations, lectures given by specialists, and on-the-job activities designed to develop knowledge of the practical aspects of trading. After this, candidates enter internships under a trader. Advancement is based on the development of each candidate and opportunities that arise as a result of the firm's expansion plans.

O'Connor looks for BAs and MBAs with strong mathematical skills. The firm would not disclose salary information. Benefits include health and dental coverage, life and disability insurance, and tuition reimbursement.

Paine Webber, Inc.

Blythe Eastman Paine Webber
1221 Avenue of the Americas
New York, New York 10020
(212) 730-8500

Paine Webber Mitchell Hutchins
140 Broadway
New York, New York 10005
(212) 437-2121

Paine Webber Jackson Curtis
140 Broadway
New York, New York 10005
(212) 437-2121

Confused by all the names above? Well, don't be. Paine Webber is actually a holding company for all its operating divisions. Blythe Eastman Paine Webber is the investment banking arm, Paine Webber Jackson Curtis is the retail bro-

160

kerage operation, and Paine Webber Mitchell Hutchins encompasses the securities research department, institutional salesforce, and asset management department. Overall, Paine Webber is the tenth largest securities firm in the United States.

Blythe Eastman Paine Webber is particularly strong in public finance, providing financing and advisory services to states, municipalities, and other government authorities. The public finance department works on everything from sewer projects to sports stadiums. This department, which is a growth area for the firm, hires from five to ten MBA associates a year.

Upon joining the firm, new associates spend from two to three months with sales, trading, and underwriting professionals in the municipal bond department. Here, new hires gain an understanding of the tax-exempt market, get a feel for who the players are, and learn about the economic, political, and social forces that "move the market." After this rotational assignment, associates are permanently placed in a specialist group, although they are expected to develop the technical and banking skills of a generalist. Responsibilities of the associate include analyzing and developing new financing techniques, providing clients with investment banking advice, marketing the firm's services to potential clients, assisting in the drafting of documents, gathering market data, developing marketing materials, and providing computer support for cash flow, debt scheduling, arbitrage, and yield analysis.

The firm prefers MBAs who have at least two years of prior work experience, who can handle pressure-cooker situations, and who don't mind traveling.

Paine Webber Mitchell Hutchins hires MBAs and/or individuals with at least two years of prior experience as sales associates and sales traders in the institutional equity sales and trading department. The firm prefers those with marketing and finance backgrounds. The formal six-month training program for this division is designed to give the trainee a solid understanding of the securities industry.

The firm considers this program the most comprehensive of its kind on Wall Street. Trainees spend time with securities analysts, traders, brokers, sales representatives, options specialists, syndicate managers, and senior management. After these rotations, each trainee enters into an apprenticeship, acting as a partner to a senior staff member on certain accounts. At the end of the program, trainees receive a list of well-established accounts of their own.

The firm would not disclose salary or benefits information.

Salomon Brothers, Inc.
One New York Plaza
New York, New York 10004
(212) 747-7000

Founded in 1910 as a partnership, Salomon Brothers merged with Phillip Brothers, the commodities traders, in 1981 and is now a wholly owned subsidiary of Phibro-Salomon, Inc. Although "Solly" is technically a public firm, it still retains a sense of partnership, and senior managers are still referred to as "The Brothers." Solly is the second-largest securities firm in the United States, behind Merrill Lynch, and was the leading underwriter in 1983. The firm is also known for its excellent bond department. Henry Kaufman, long considered the wiseman of Wall Street, calls Solly his home.

The firm has a reputation for innovation and is a market leader in many respects. Employees characterize the work atmosphere at Solly as "highly charged." One remarked, "If you can make it at Solly, you can make it anywhere on The Street."

The only problem with Solly is that it's a very hard place to get into. In 1983 the firm screened over 13,000 résumés, gave interviews to 800 applicants, and hired 60 people. Of these, approximately half went into sales and trading, with the other half going into corporate finance. New hires in these two areas go through classroom training together because both groups are required to sit for, and pass, the Series Seven exam. Courses begin in August, last for four weeks, and are videotaped so that participants can review them. Subjects covered include government securities, money markets, mortgage-backed securities, equities, and corporate finance. Exams are administered at the end of each week, and they are taken quite seriously. The Series Seven exam is taken within two months of the classes.

After passing the exam, those in the sales and trading area

have to "find" themselves jobs. There is a slot for everyone hired, but individuals must seek out areas that interest them and convince the vice presidents heading them that they deserve to be hired. The firm's priorities are matched with those of the trainees' as much as possible, but if Solly needs you somewhere, don't be surprised if that's where you end up! Keep in mind, however, that these assignments are not necessarily permanent. Employees are expected to move within the firm during their careers.

After the Series Seven exam, the corporate finance associates attend one week of seminars given by two vice presidents on various technical topics, such as spread sheets, word processing, and dividend studies. Afterward, they are assigned to their first account teams and serve as generalists for two years or so.

Solly also hires fifteen to twenty BA analysts per year, for a two-year stay. Most go into the corporate finance department. Training consists of a one-week orientation to the firm, after which analysts are pretty much on their own. Senior people are helpful, but they don't "spoon feed" analysts.

In corporate finance, salaries start at approximately $25,000 for BAs and $45,000 for MBAs. The figures are somewhat less for salespeople and traders. Benefits include major medical and dental coverage, life insurance, reduced stock commissions, stock purchase plan, and tuition reimbursement.

6 / *Accounting Firms*

Some people still confuse accountants with bookkeepers. But the public accounting profession has come a long way since the days when men in green eyeshades were hunched over adding machines in back offices. Today accounting is as prestigious a profession as architecture or law. Accountants are the experts in the very language of business, and they help American corporations, as well as individuals and governments, report their financial condition and manage their money.

The leading accounting firms in the nation are collectively referred to as the Big Eight. They are: Arthur Andersen, Coopers & Lybrand, Deloitte Haskins & Sells, Ernst & Whinney, Peat Marwick Mitchell, Price Waterhouse, Arthur Young, and Touche Ross. The Big Eight firms audit about 75 percent to 80 percent of all companies registered with the SEC. Following closely in the footsteps of their multinational corporate clients, they operate all over the globe.

SERVICES TO CUSTOMERS

Auditing

The core function of accounting is auditing. Accountants are hired by firms to study their financial statements and render an independent judgment as to their accuracy and fairness. A stamp of approval from a major accounting firm can be a very important asset to a company. If corporations want to register with the SEC in order to issue public debt or equity, or even if they want to apply for a bank loan, they must present audited financial statements that adhere to the accounting principles appropriate for a given industry. These generally accepted accounting principles—GAAP* as they are commonly called—are outlined by the Financial Accounting Standards Board (FASB), a prestigious organization comprising seven CPAs appointed by the trustees of the American Institute of Certified Public Accountants (AICPA). Members of the FASB serve staggered five-year sessions, and they can serve for only two terms. In addition, they must disassociate themselves from former employers in order to maintain their independence. An FASB decision to change an accounting principle very often has a major impact on the business community.

The accountant's "opinion" of a company's financial statements always appears in the annual report and is either "qualified" or "unqualified." An unqualified opinion means that the auditor feels that the company's report accurately reflects the true condition of the firm. A qualified opinion means that the auditor has some doubt about the report's accuracy and/ or thoroughness. Obviously, companies don't want to have an officially qualified opinion. When auditors challenge a report's presentation, therefore, a company will generally institute the changes required to make it acceptable under the unqualified category.

Most firms conduct audit engagements* handled by an "engagement team." A partner usually heads the team, supported by managers, supervisors, seniors, and staff accountants. At the conclusion of the audit engagement, the accounting firm will send a "management letter" to the client, outlining the results of its findings and identifying any problem areas uncovered in the course of the audit. Many times, the accounting firm will offer advice as to how these problems might be cleared up.

Proper financial reporting is extremely important because the investment community makes very significant decisions on

165

the basis of financial records generated by companies. There have been a number of controversial incidents in recent years in which companies misled the public by manipulating their results to make sales and earnings look better. Accounting firms have been known to sign off on financial statements of companies that had engaged in mismanagement and, on some occasions, fraud. In 1982, for example, one of the Big Eight got into a little trouble with a certain computer manufacturer. It seems that the company's marketing department, anxious to show increased sales, resorted to some questionable accounting practices. After an internal investigation, the company was forced to revise its earnings by about $15 million in one quarter.

In some cases, accountants are held responsible for not doing their jobs properly. By definition, however, accountants lead a split existence: On the one hand, they are paid by their client corporations; on the other hand, they have a responsibility of great magnitude to the public. This is why the profession is called public accounting.

Most companies have their own internal auditors who manage financial reporting and accounting systems. When accountants work for a corporation instead of an accounting concern, it is called private accounting. When an accounting firm comes in to review the finances of Fortune 500 companies, it is, in many cases, auditing the auditors. This is not the case with smaller companies, where outside auditors must review the basic accounting systems of the firms as well as the specific numbers. Auditing smaller companies may very well be more complicated and more time-consuming than auditing larger companies, which are more sophisticated and which may not be as open to suggestions from the outside.

In fact, providing service to smaller businesses is considered a high-growth area by many accounting firms. The number of new corporations expected to be registered with the SEC, and thus to require the services of an auditor, is projected to slow down. At the same time, smaller firms are being deluged by increasingly complex financial reporting requirements. Accounting firms would like to help these "emerging growth companies," not only by doing their audits but also by serving as broad-based consultants. Today, computerization has made auditing less expensive and more efficient than ever before. Paradoxically, therefore, auditing is not seen as a big growth area within accounting firms, because it has basically become a commodity business, as have straight commercial bank loans. Many accounting companies have been diversifying and concentrating on operations like tax planning and consulting, which offer more potential for growth.

Tax Services

Accountants are very active in helping companies and individuals with tax planning and tax returns. Nobody likes filing a tax return, but if you think an individual return is complicated, consider what General Motors' is like.

In the United States, corporations are permitted to maintain two sets of financial records (or "books," as they are called): one for eventual public disclosure in the annual report and one for submission to the Internal Revenue Service (IRS). Different accounting rules apply to each set of books, and in many cases the differences allow the corporation to pay lower taxes because the "book" sent to the IRS usually shows less income than does the annual report.

Through their tax consulting operations, accountants help a corporation interpret tax statutes with an eye toward keeping its tax bill as low as possible. They advise on internal changes within the company—such as corporate reorganizations, methods of valuing inventory, and international investment—that may have particular significance from a tax point of view. The tax department in an accounting firm may also represent clients in the event of any disputes with the IRS.

Consulting

Many of the larger accounting firms have management consulting units, that develop information systems for corporate clients. For instance, consultants may help devise a one-year, five-year, or ten-year business plan for a firm. Then they will help build systems for reporting all the information needed to support the plan.

Unlike management consulting firms like Booz Allen and the Boston Consulting Group, much of the consulting done in accounting firms is computer-related. As a result, many firms have computer specialists who customize software packages to suit the individual requirements of the client. Consultants may also be brought in to study and report on a specific problem area—for instance, the implications of overseas investment for a multinational company.

JOB OPPORTUNITIES

According to industry statistics, the accounting profession is growing faster than almost any other segment of the economy. In addition, accounting firms run some of the most highly respected training programs of all financial institutions. This may be due in part to the fact that accountants need to keep constantly abreast of changes in their field. In some accounting firms, each employee is required to take part in a specified amount of training each year (at Arthur Andersen, about 10 percent of an officer's time is spent in class). Many accounting firms run "mini-universities" and offer a wide variety of courses on a regular basis. Some even have their own publishing businesses that print instructional materials as well as the firm's interpretations on new FASB rulings or developments in the business community.

Accounting firms hire most of their new employees at the entry level, whether for auditing, tax planning, or consulting. It takes about two years to advance from a staff accountant position to the senior accountant level.

Most of the opportunities for BAs are in auditing. Candidates are usually required to pass an exam to become a CPA (certified public accountant). The exam is made up of four parts—theory of accounts, accounting problems, auditing, and commercial law—and lasts for two and a half days.

A beginning job in auditing may not make for the most stimulating work. Typically, trainees have responsibility for minute details, such as counting inventory and checking to ensure that serial numbers on bond certificates correspond to those that were pledged as security at an earlier date. The increasing use of computers in the profession, however, has alleviated the tedium somewhat and will continue to do so in the future. The value of the entry-level auditing job is the training received and the experience gained in how corporations truly work—from the ground up. For someone who does not know anything about business, an accounting training program may be the best way to find out.

Some of the accounting firms do hire BAs directly into their tax departments, but they usually look for those with an undergraduate degree in accounting. The ideal candidate has an undergraduate degree in accounting plus an MBA, a law degree, or a master's degree in taxation. Tax specialists are also usually required to pass the CPA exam.

Consulting is probably the fastest-growing area in accounting firms. Trainees recruited into consulting usually have an MBA or an advanced degree in another specialty, such as computers or engineering, in addition to some full-time work experience. Firms that emphasize computerized systems may hire college grads at the entry level if they have strong computer or technical backgrounds. In this business, credibility is extremely important. After all, companies are usually seeking advice for problems that cannot be managed internally. Consulting firms look for candidates who have experience with the industries and/or projects that they will cover as a consultant. In many accounting firms, however, it is possible to move into consulting after getting a foot in the door by working in the tax or auditing departments.

Serving smaller businesses is a good place for fledgling entrepreneurs to get started. Accountants go out in the field with their customers and help them "grow" their businesses: What better background for starting your own business than helping others begin theirs and having the benefit of all their mistakes?

One of the most compelling reasons to join an accounting firm is the lure of future partnership. All the Big Eight firms are privately held, so that profits accrue directly to the partners. A partner has total responsibility for handling specific client relationships and ensuring that the standards of the firm are met. Partnerships are not given to everyone. It usually takes between eight and twelve years to make partner, during which time candidates undergo a long series of evaluations and interviews and a tough weeding-out process. Job opportunities for those who don't make partner are quite good and often lucrative. Many former accountants can be found in the controller's office of corporations—a few years' experience in a good accounting firm is extremely valuable to companies who need internal people to handle accounting issues. They may also become corporate financial analysts or move to a smaller accounting firm.

MASTER OF SCIENCE PROGRAM IN ACCOUNTING

A number of accounting firms in New York City offer an interesting opportunity for liberal arts majors with little or no exposure to the accounting profession. The accounting firm pays them a salary while they go to business school at night and in the summers to get a master of science degree in accounting. One program of this type is offered at New York University. Approximately 50 candidates a year are chosen to participate. The program begins in the summer with three months of full-time course work at NYU. Candidates may also attend a formal orientation program at their sponsoring firms. In the fall and spring, trainees work full time at the accounting firm and go to NYU two nights a week. During the second summer, they attend NYU full time once again, for the most intensive part of the program. When the program is finished, candidates can opt to obtain an MBA by taking just a few extra courses.

The sequence of coursework in the MS program is as follows:

Summer 1   Fundamentals of Financial Accounting
               Managerial Accounting
               Statistics and Quantitative Methods

Fall-Spring	Financial Accounting Theory (Intermediate and Advanced)
	Financial Accounting Policy
	Auditing
	Corporate Financial Management
Summer 2	Information Systems
	Managerial Accounting (Internal Reporting Control)
	Business Law
	Federal Income Taxes
	Financial Markets

All of the Big Eight firms, as well as Main Hurdman, have participated in this program. Similar opportunities are available in Boston in conjunction with Northeastern University and in Hartford, with the University of Hartford. Programs may also be available in Chicago, Los Angeles, Dallas, and Houston.

Alexander Grant & Company
3900 Prudential Plaza
Chicago, Illinois 60601
(312) 856-0001

Alexander Grant is an accounting firm that specializes in serving middle-market customers. Headquartered in Chicago, the firm has over 60 offices in major cities in the United States. The offices are much smaller than those of the Big Eight firms. The firm hires into the accounting and auditing, tax, and consulting areas at the entry level.

On a national basis, Alexander Grant hires approximately 200 people into its accounting and auditing division each year. Upon joining the firm, auditors take an introductory auditing course and then six to eight months later, a course on managerial and supervisory skills. The firm also provides self-study guides to help auditors pass the CPA exam.

The tax department at Alexander Grant is growing rapidly. Each year it accepts 20 people, including BAs and MBAs as well as some transfers from the auditing department. All professionals are required to take 40 hours of continuing education a year.

Salaries vary across the nation. As a point of reference, BAs in New York start at between $18,000 and $20,000 with MBAs beginning at around $25,000. Benefits include medical coverage and an overtime bank that can be used for extra vacation.

Arthur Andersen & Company
1345 Avenue of the Americas
New York, New York 10019
(212) 708-4000
Locations in every major city in the U.S. and abroad.
Contact the location nearest you.

Arthur Andersen, one of the Big Eight, is a huge company, with over 25,000 employees staffing 75 offices in major U.S. cities and in 42 countries. The consulting operation alone constitutes the largest of its kind in the world. Arthur Andersen audits more companies on the New York and American stock exchanges than any other firm.

Almost everyone at Arthur Andersen starts at the bottom. For this reason, the firm is very active in campus recruiting activities, looking for candidates to begin careers in auditing, tax, and consulting.

More BAs are hired into the auditing areas than MBAs—many trainees report that BAs comprise around 80 percent of their group. Training begins in Firmwide Audit Staff Training School. The first week is spent in the home office getting acquainted. Trainees are then sent to Arthur Andersen's Center for Professional Education in St. Charles, Illinois (near Chicago). The center is like a college campus, with a residence hall that houses 700 people, computer facilities, video rooms, a cafeteria, a bar, softball, basketball, Ping-Pong—the works. All trainees, regardless of what area they are in, spend some time at the school in order to meet and work with other members of the firm's worldwide staff. For auditors, the big assignment during the two-week stay is a complete audit of a dummy company using transaction flow auditing (TFA), the buzzword for AA's auditing procedures.

In addition to the initial three-week course, the firm offers self-study materials to prepare trainees for the CPA exam. As with all accounting firms, a certain amount of training is required each year. This may range from one-day courses on specific auditing techniques to five-day seminars that demand substantial preparation. Much of the entry-level training is on the job, and according to the firm, a new staff member may be involved in as many as ten audits in the first year.

In the tax area, Arthur Andersen hires BAs, BSs, MBAs, MSs, LLMs, and JDs, (did we leave anything out?), all with experience in accounting, business, taxation, or law. All new hires without advanced degrees must pass the CPA exam. Shortly after joining the firm, new hires spend three weeks in St. Charles taking a tax course. Classes are taught by internal staff. Subsequent coursework is structured to meet the employee's needs.

Arthur Andersen's management information consulting operation is a real growth area for the company. The staff now numbers around 5,000 and is still growing. The consulting area hires a diverse group for a three- or four-year training process. Arthur Andersen is one of the few accounting firms that hires BAs with technical backgrounds directly into the consulting function. Shortly after joining the company, consultants spend three weeks training at the St. Charles facility. One consultant told us that to prepare for this session he had to do six months of schoolwork in three weeks. Trainees are introduced to computer systems, including COBOL and data structures, as well as to the company's methodology.

After this, consulting trainees begin working on client assignments. Experiences during this period are designed to enhance their knowledge of computers and data collection techniques. Beginning consultants also undertake rigorous self-study programs, complete with workbooks and proficiency exams that must be passed before they are qualified to charge time to the unit.

Arthur Andersen would not disclose salary information. BA trainees we spoke with reported starting salaries of approximately $20,000, with MBAs starting in the mid-twenties. Benefits include partial medical and dental coverage and life insurance. Two weeks of vacation are given, but overtime can be accumulated for up to two additional weeks of vacation.

Coopers & Lybrand
National Recruiting Department
1251 Avenue of the Americas
New York, New York 10020
(212) 489-1100

Coopers & Lybrand has offices in over 90 locations in the United States. A member of the Big Eight, the firm considers itself a market leader in computerized auditing methods and has also made a substantial investment in career guidance, hiring a staff of 150 specifically for this purpose. Because C&L's recruiting is decentralized, the director of national recruiting recommends contacting local offices directly for job openings.

Most new hires at the firm begin in auditing, which takes in approximately 1,300 people a year. Of this amount, 85 percent are BAs or BSs and the remaining 15 percent are MBAs. The firm likes candidates who are comfortable with computers, but they needn't be programming wizards.

After two weeks of preliminary classroom instruction, audit training is essentially on the job. The first week consists of an orientation to the firm, its policies, and procedures. In the next week, new hires learn the firm's auditing techniques and how to use the computer system. Further training courses depend on what types of industries the auditor is working on. The firm estimates that first-year auditors take an average of 80 additional hours in training over the course of the year. Structured training programs are given in subsequent years as well, each designed to teach the employee the skills required at different levels of responsibility. All employees are required to take a minimum of 40 hours per year of formalized training. C&L encourages people not to specialize in the first year or two but rather to get a broad array of experiences. First promotions come six to fifteen months after joining the firm, and employees are reviewed after every 40-hour period of engagement work. Auditors are required to pass the CPA exam and are given self-study courses for this purpose.

C&L hires approximately 175 people a year into the tax division, approximately 75 percent of whom have law degrees. Auditors with one to two years of experience may be given the opportunity to transfer into tax if they so desire. In the beginning, new hires take courses on business tax concepts, the firm's tax practice, and how to use the Internal Revenue Code and regulations. Tax professionals then study tax accruals, Subchapter C of the Internal Revenue Code, and consolidated tax returns. They also attend an annual tax conference consisting of workshops and general meetings on tax-law changes, tax planning methods, and other areas of interest. Members of the tax staff also attend seminars on their specialty area.

The consulting area is not a major hirer at C&L. Each year it accepts only about 25 people firmwide, either MBAs or individuals with five to ten years of work experience. The firm considers itself to be quite strong in health care consulting.

There are opportunities for overseas assignments after three to four years of domestic experience. The firm also has an actuarial benefits consulting group that hires about twenty BAs and BSs per year. This division helps large and medium-size corporate clients set up benefits programs and package them for employees.

Salaries vary with geographic location. As a point of reference, in New York BAs start at $18,000 to $22,000, with MBAs starting anywhere from $24,000 to $38,000. The higher levels for MBAs are usually for consultants. Benefits include Blue Cross/Blue Shield, life insurance, firm-sponsored IRAs, and an overtime bank that can be used for extra vacation time.

Deloitte Haskins & Sells
1114 Avenue of the Americas
New York, New York 10036
(212) 790-0500

One of the Big Eight, DH&S has over 100 offices in the United States and over 19,000 employees. The firm believes that entry-level professionals should pass the CPA exam as soon as possible. To this end, it publishes a series of CPA review guides in self-study form. In-house study sessions are arranged or employees are encouraged to take a CPA review course, with the firm picking up the tab.

First-year auditors are required to take courses in auditing procedures and accounting concepts. The auditing class is a one-week seminar that provides a general introduction to GAAP and to auditing as it is conducted at DH&S. The accounting concepts class is taken after six to eight months with the firm. It is designed to review the trainee's on-the-job experience and discuss any problems encountered. These two courses are supplemented with sessions on accounting techniques in specialized industries.

New hires in the tax department usually have an advanced degree in accounting or taxation. Entry-level training begins with a one-week orientation seminar similar to the introduction for auditors. After spending one "busy season" with the firm (January to April), tax professionals take a two-week intermediate program on tax laws and their applications, tax regulation, and precedent-setting court cases. The basic training is supplemented with seminars on such topics as tax computer applications, depreciation, and partnerships.

Most new hires in management consulting have MBAs or work experience, and training varies with past experience. New hires go through the basic program with the auditing staff, while those transferring from the auditing division go directly into the more advanced classes. Initial courses are held in principles of information systems, writing for the consulting environment, systems design, financial modeling, human resources planning, production and inventory control, organization planning, and group communications skills.

These basic courses are supplemented with specialized industry seminars hosted by the auditing division.

Salaries are competitive within local markets. In New York, for example, salaries begin in the low twenties for BAs and high twenties to mid-thirties for those with advanced degrees. Benefits include health insurance, life insurance, and pension plan. Overtime can be accumulated toward extra vacation.

Ernst & Whinney   **International Headquarters**
(National Office)   **153 East 53rd Street**
2000 National City Center   **New York, New York 10022**
Cleveland, Ohio 44114   **(212) 888-9100**
(216) 861-5000

Ernst & Whinney is one of the Big Eight and operates over 300 offices in 70 countries around the world. The majority of E&W's clients are in manufacturing, although the financial services, high-technology, energy, and health care industries have been high growth areas for the firm.

Ernst & Whinney's training for auditors takes place mainly on the job. In their first year, new hires may work on anywhere from ten to fifteen different client engagements in a variety of industries. Work experience is supplemented by classes held at various regional sites across the country. Auditors participate in the new accountants program, the staff accountants program, and accounting, auditing, and tax. Trainees also participate in an introductory program for new tax staff that relies on a variety of teaching methods, including case studies, audiovisual aids, and computer techniques. Candidates are encouraged to pass the CPA exam as soon as possible, and E&W provides a CPA review course to this end.

Over the next two years new auditors may take further courses in advanced auditing techniques, specialized industries, and communications skills. In addition, intermittent seminars are held on current developments in the field.

Ernst & Whinney considers its tax professional development program to be the most extensive in the profession. The firm likes to hire people with law degrees and claims that its training is the equivalent of a master's in taxation program.

177

Training courses are held over a three-year period at the firm's national tax department in Washington, D.C. In the first year, new hires take part in the new tax staff program and attend seminars on current tax developments. They also take the CPA review course, because anyone aspiring to partner level must have a CPA. In the second year, tax professionals take national tax training, which covers such areas as corporate tax and family financial planning. They also take a course designed to improve writing skills. In the third year, tax staff members take courses on specialized industries and advanced topics in taxation.

Like many accounting firms, Ernst & Whinney has a consulting operation that hires people with graduate degrees in accounting, computer science, hospital and public administration, engineering, and planning. The firm also looks for candidates with significant work experience. E&W takes an individualized approach to training its consulting staff. Training courses are offered internally, but the firm will also pay for any outside courses that are deemed appropriate. As in other areas of the firm, basic training is really a three-year process. First-year classes cover consultant orientation, writing skills, and technical update seminars. In the second year, consultants take part in financial modeling classes and specialized industry workshops. In the third year, the focus is on marketing and management skills. Opportunities are available for overseas assignments or transfers among domestic offices. The firm maintains that moves are not forced.

Due to the great differences between salary levels in different locations, the firm did not give us salary information. Benefits include life insurance, health and accident insurance, pension plan, and up to 80 overtime hours of extra vacation time.

Fox & Co.
2700 Lincoln Center Building
Denver, Colorado 80264
(303) 831-9596

Fox is the twelfth largest accounting firm in the United States with over 55 domestic offices. Its strength lies in servicing middle-market companies with sales of between $1 million and $50 million. Nationwide, Fox hires between 275 and 325 entry-level professionals every year. Approximately 90 percent to 95 percent of these have undergraduate degrees and start in the auditing department. Recently, however, Fox has moved toward starting people directly in one of its two other areas—tax and business advisory services.

First-year auditors take a national-level training program held at the University of Colorado in Boulder. This training segment lasts seven or eight days and covers an introduction to the firm, Fox's auditing methods, and communication skills. Advanced topics are covered through a series of district seminars on specialized industries and new accounting rules. During their first year, auditors work on eight to twelve engagements as part of a team of three to six people. At the conclusion of the first year, they attend courses in more advanced accounting topics as well as the drafting of financial statements.

According to a spokesman for Fox, the firm does more direct hiring into tax and business advisory services (which accepts a number of MBAs) than most other accounting firms. Training for these two areas overlaps with parts of the auditing program. In addition, the firm has a special study arrangement with Colorado State University that is comparable to a master's in taxation program. All employees taking the CPA exam are given time off to prepare, and those who pass it receive a $400 to $500 bonus.

Nationwide salaries average $19,000 for BAs and $28,000 for those with graduate degrees. Benefits include major medical and dental coverage and life insurance. In addition, up to 80 hours of overtime can be used toward vacation. Anything over 80 hours is paid out in salary.

Laventhol & Horwath
1845 Walnut Street
Philadelphia, Pennsylvania 19103
(215) 299-1600

Although smaller than the Big Eight firms, Laventhol & Horwath has a very sizable accounting practice. Most new hires begin in the auditing area but may switch within two years into some other area, such as tax or consulting.

Training begins with a six-day orientation to the firm and its policies. Entry-level audit trainees then participate in two days of workshops on the ins and outs of individual and corporate tax returns and the fundamentals of tax research, including computer-aided research methods. A course is also given in EDP concepts to familiarize trainees with computer terminology, operations, and applications in the accounting profession.

The firm also provides a self-study course for the CPA exam. Throughout training, "what's new" meetings are held to keep employees up to date on new pronouncements, emerging issues in accounting or taxes, or changes in the firm's policies or procedures. All professional employees are required to take a minimum of 40 hours of training each year.

The firm would not disclose salary information, except to say they are competitive within their markets. Benefits include life insurance, travel accident insurance, comprehensive hospital insurance, surgical and major medical coverage, profit sharing, and tuition reimbursement.

Main Hurdman
Park Avenue Plaza
55 East 52nd Street
New York, New York 10055
(212) 909-5000

Main Hurdman likes to think of itself as a member of the "Big Nine"—big enough to serve the needs of large customers but small enough to encourage a sense of independence in its employees. Nationwide, the firm employs over 3,500 people, roughly 500 of whom are partners. This is supplemented by MH's international arm: Klynveld, Main Goerdeler (KMG), the largest accounting firm in the European Economic Community. Main Hurdman's primary business remains auditing, but following an industry trend, it is expanding its involvement in tax and consulting.

In 1984, the firm filled 350 entry-level openings. Approximately 75 percent of trainees are hired in the auditing area as staff accountants, and 80 percent to 90 percent have under-graduate degrees in accounting. In their first year, auditors spend at least 80 hours in the classroom, with the balance covered by on-the-job training. The core course is the audit-ing orientation program, which lasts one week and is taught by members of the firm. It is a basic introduction to the firm and its auditing techniques. The program is supplemented by shorter courses in practical areas such as cost accounting, in-ventory accounting, and microcomputer techniques.

First-year auditing responsibilities vary from office to office. As a rule, the smaller the office, the broader the exposure to clients and different aspects of auditing. Smaller offices con-centrate on middle-market firms and thus offer a wider range of audit engagements over the course of a year. The initial experience is heavily concentrated on detail work; the larger the client, the more specific the audit. Staff auditors compile information for experienced staff accountants who are charged with such responsibilities as drafting balance sheets. The quality of the experience depends on the supervisor's involvement and how much responsibility new auditors are prepared to handle.

After completing one or two audits with the firm, trainees attend a one-week series of lectures, case studies, and presen-tations designed to teach ratio analysis, basic EDP concepts, techniques for interviewing clients, and introductory tax ac-counting. After this phase of the program, auditors gain ad-ditional line responsibilities, and within ten to sixteen months move into a supervisory role. Auditors are expected to sit for the CPA exam during their first months with the firm. While MH doesn't offer specific in-house courses, it does provide self-directed study guides for the exam.

Main Hurdman's tax area, which now represents only 20 percent of the firm's revenues, is growing rapidly. Most open-ings are filled by MBAs, JDs, or people who have spent a few years in auditing; however, some BAs are hired directly. Entry-level members of the department are given a one-week introductory course on income tax accounting and research. The balance of the first year is spent on the job and is supple-mented by seminars on specific tax-related issues.

Management consulting represents MH's newest and smallest operation. Consultants may be just out of business school, may have spent two years auditing, or may have substantial work experience. They are given an introductory seminar lasting about three days and spend the rest of training primarily on the job.

Salaries vary across the country. As a point of reference, BAs in New York start at $20,000, with MBAs starting from $23,000 to $25,000. Benefits include major medical coverage, life insurance, and an overtime bank.

Peat Marwick Mitchell & Co.
345 Park Avenue
New York, New York 10154
(212) 758-9700

Peat Marwick, the North American operation of Peat Marwick International, is one of the Big Eight. Founded in 1897, the firm currently employs 22,000 professionals in 100 offices nationwide.

PM interviewed over 18,000 applicants in 1983. Every one of the interviews was performed either by a partner or by a line manager—an indication of management's active involvement in the recruiting process. Approximately 6,000 applicants had second interviews, over 4,000 received offers, and 2,000 accepted. The recruiting season lasts from mid-September through March, with the heaviest work done in the early portion of the schedule.

According to company sources, Peat Marwick puts more emphasis on national recruiting than some of the other accounting firms. So if you are an accounting student in Boston, do not hesitate to tell the recruiter you are interested in the Houston office. If a specific office makes an offer, it is not automatically transferable to another location. Most interviewers demand that applicants be up front with them. If you impress a recruiter, his or her recommendation lends instant credibility to your application to the other office.

All entry-level employees take a five-day orientation seminar that includes an introduction to how the firm uses the Macintosh computer for accounting applications. The balance of the program is spent introducing specific services offered by PM and what entry-level employees can expect in their first year of job training.

Most entry-level staffers come in as auditors. After two to three months of on-the-job assignments, they return to the classroom for an auditing seminar designed to prepare them to assume greater workloads. This one-week course covers PM's approach to auditing, sampling techniques, revenue, purchasing and production cycles, and financial statement presentation. New auditors are expected to sit for the CPA exam soon after joining. PM has its own study program, but those who choose to take an outside "recognized" review program qualify for two-thirds tuition reimbursement when they pass the exam.

Within twelve to eighteen months of joining the firm, auditors take the "in-charge seminar," a week-long program designed to help them assume greater responsibility on the auditing team. Topics covered include responsibilities of an in-charge auditor, planning and administering auditing engagements, audit sampling techniques and plans, and inventory auditing.

Since many auditors either leave the firm or move to a different area within the organization, an advanced in-charge seminar is given to those who are prepared to make a longer-term commitment to auditing (usually after two and a half or three years with the firm). The seminar, which lasts thirteen days and brings auditors from throughout the firm together in a central location, covers business and management skills, auditing and financial reporting, strategic planning, auditing theory, strategy and efficiency, styles of effective supervision, and professional conduct.

Almost half the entry-level positions in tax are filled by auditors with two years of experience. The balance are filled by candidates with graduate degrees or by professionals with extensive tax backgrounds, such as former IRS agents. Much of the training in tax is self-directed; however, entry-level tax accountants do go through the orientation seminar. The first year of tax training is highlighted by a one-week seminar on basic tax concepts that examines how various tax statutes affect particular types of firms and how to prepare the necessary tax forms.

Management consulting comprises roughly 25 percent of PM's overall business, but it is an area in which the firm is making a concerted effort to grow. The result is that PM is actively recruiting at most of the top business schools in the country. Positions in consulting are also filled by transfers from either auditing or tax. PM's private business advisory services group, which brings all the firm's services under one umbrella, also falls under the heading of management consulting.

Consultants are expected to have considerable experience when they join the firm. Nevertheless, they are given detailed training by the firm on an ongoing basis. A week-long skills workshop introduces the basics of consulting and covers techniques for gathering and interpreting data, formulating recommendations, and presenting reports to clients.

Salaries in major cities begin in the low twenties for BAs and high twenties to mid-thirties for MBAs. Benefits include major medical and dental coverage, life insurance, reduced loan rates, credit cards, nine-month maternity leave, and time and a half for overtime, which can be accumulated for vacation or salary.

Price Waterhouse
1251 Avenue of the Americas
New York, New York 10020
(212) 489-8900

Price Waterhouse, considered the Morgan Guaranty of the Big Eight accounting firms, maintains offices in over 80 countries. PW's extensive activities abroad make it a logical choice for those seeking some overseas work experience. In the United States, PW has over 70 offices. Price Waterhouse has gained some public recognition and TV exposure as the firm that helps keep the Academy Awards "the most honest election in the world"!

Most people at PW begin their careers in auditing. When new hires come into this division, they spend three weeks in classes. Basic auditing techniques are presented through case studies culled from live client situations. During this time, computer applications are also introduced. Training then continues on the job, where new hires join an engagement team as staff accountants. Job assignments usually focus in on audits of cash, accounts payable, payrolls, fixed assets, and prepaid and accrued items. After each engagement, trainees receive a written evaluation prepared by their immediate supervisor.

During their on-the-job experience, new hires are encouraged to participate in a disciplined reading program in order to learn as much about the accounting profession and the business world as they can. PW also offers a two-volume self-study guide to help staff members prepare for the CPA exam. After a year with the firm, auditors take a 40-hour intermediate auditing course as well as courses in advanced audit testing techniques, audit program development, income tax concepts, and writing skills.

Most of PW's tax staff are transfers from the auditing division, although the firm does accept some individuals as direct hires. All new tax professionals receive training in the firm's policies and procedures and standards for systems development. For five days, new hires work on case studies and spend some time building their communications skills. They also receive technical training in computer programming, design and documentation, modeling, and installation.

Like most accounting firms, PW requires all professional staff members to take a minimum of 20 hours of classes per year and 120 hours over a three-year period. When employees reach the senior accountant level, usually after two to three years with the firm, they can apply for an overseas assignment. Service tours of up to two and a half years are offered in Britain, Europe, South America, Australia, and the Far East. At the end of the tour participants may remain in the foreign office or return to the United States.

Price Waterhouse would not disclose salary information. Benefits include medical insurance, overtime bank, professional expenses for certification, CPA coaching course reimbursement (75 percent maximum, to $500).

Seidman & Seidman
15 Columbus Circle
New York, New York 10023
(212) 765-7500

Seidman & Seidman (pronounced Seedman and Seedman) is part of an international partnership—Binder Dijker Otte & Co.—the world's tenth largest accounting firm. The company considers its tax practice to be very strong, along with the services it provides to middle-market companies. S&S boasts a number of well-known figures in the accounting profession, including J. S. Seidman, former chairman of the AICPA (American Institute of Certified Public Accountants), and B. Z. Lee, who was recently named new chairman of the AICPA.

S&S's offices tend to be smaller than those of the Big Eight, and its partner-to-staff ratio is about one to five, as compared with one to ten at some of the larger firms. The firm hires BAs, JDs, and MBAs every year. Queries should be sent to the partner-in-charge at the location where the applicant wishes to work. Call the central number for a current list of this information.

New hires begin in either the auditing or tax areas. Although the firm could not provide us with nationwide hiring numbers, they did say that in New York, which is one of their largest offices, they made 25 auditor and 2 new tax hires. Upon joining the firm, everyone is assigned to an adviser, who is a partner. All trainees participate in a two-day self-study "Introduction to Seidman & Seidman" course, which covers the firm's policies and procedures. All entry-level employees then go on to a week-long introductory course covering auditing methods and corporate and individual income taxes. The course requires about 40 hours of advance preparation. Other courses offered to new hires include communications skills, management development, and SEC accounting. The firm also provides paid time off for preparation for the CPA exam.

New employees in the tax department take a tax course designed to help them develop good tax research methods and to increase their knowledge of the principles of individual and corporate taxation. In addition to these entry-level requirements, all CPAs must take 20 hours a year and 120 hours every three years of continuing professional education. Special industry courses are also administered according to the employee's area of concentration. All training is done by in-house personnel.

Salaries in New York start between $19,000 and $21,000. Benefits include hospital insurance, medical and surgical insurance, life insurance, investment and retirement plan, paid overtime or additional vacation days, and tuition reimbursement evaluated on an individual basis.

Touche Ross
1633 Broadway
New York, New York 10019
(212) 489-1600

In terms of staff, Touche Ross is one of the smaller members of the Big Eight. It operates offices in major cities across the United States. Interested candidates should contact the office at which they would like to be assigned.

The firm hires around 725 people a year, 75 percent of whom are undergraduates with accounting backgrounds. The majority of new hires come into the auditing department. The tax department accepts 170 people a year, and the firm likes to see candidates with advanced degrees in law or taxation. The consulting area is not a large hirer at the entry level, accepting only about 35 MBAs with three to five years of significant work experience.

Most new hires for the auditing staff begin in the late summer after taking a course in preparation for the CPA exam. It is not mandatory for trainees to take the CPA course in the summer, but doing so gives them the opportunity to meet other new hires and make some contacts before their first day. When they formally join the firm, entry-level auditors take a two-week national auditing course. The first week is held at the local office and covers a general orientation to the firm. The second week is usually taught off site and consists of an introduction to the Touche Ross Audit Process (TRAP) and specialized industry considerations. Although most states require that all professional accountants take a minimum amount of continuing education each year (at Touche Ross it is 120 hours every three years), first-year auditors will easily amass 100 hours' worth of training. In addition to their coursework, auditors are rotated through a series of engagements designed to expose them to the various areas of auditing. The firm tries to avoid having the trainee look at the same aspect of the audit (for instance, accounts receivable or inventory) over and over again. Engagements usually last for three months or less.

New hires in the tax department and the consulting department go through a series of national training seminars. There is also a formalized tax transfer program whereby individuals who have been on the auditing staff for one and a half to two years can transfer into the tax department for six months. If they decide to stay in tax permanently, they then have to take outside courses in taxation for which the firm foots the bill.

Salaries vary across the nation. As a point of reference, starting salaries in New York are in the low twenties for undergraduate auditing staff members and in the mid- to high twenties for MBAs. New hires in the tax department make around $30,000, and consultants start in the low thirties to the mid-forties. Benefits include medical insurance, employee savings program, and an overtime bank (up to 80 hours can be added as vacation time at the employee's option).

7 / Diversified Financial Institutions

Diversified financial institutions, otherwise known as "financial supermarkets" or "hybrids," combine selected services traditionally provided by insurance companies, brokerage firms, investment banks, commercial banks, and real estate concerns all under one corporate roof. These multiservice companies are recent entries into the financial services industry. Most were established during the 1970s through mergers and/or acquisitions, and are continuing to evolve today. Three of the major commercial banks—Citicorp, BankAmerica, and Security Pacific—are sometimes grouped into this category. At present, the major nonbank financial supermarkets are Sears Roebuck, Prudential Insurance, Merrill Lynch, and American Express. Closing in fast on the market leaders are Travelers, TransAmerica, Aetna, J. C. Penney, American Can, John Hancock, and the Dreyfus Corporation. The accompanying table shows the range of services offered.

EVOLUTION

Financial supermarkets came into being because of changing consumer attitudes. In the high-inflation, high-interest-rate environment of the 1970s, the public began to question the merit of placing hard-earned money in traditional 5½ percent passbook savings accounts, particularly when the prime rate was 15 percent or even higher. For similar reasons, people

189

with whole-life insurance policies became concerned about the rate of return they were getting. When the stock market gained momentum in the summer of 1982, investors began to wonder why their profits were being eaten away by what appeared to be unreasonably high commission fees. In short, economic conditions were forcing consumers to develop more sophisticated ways of managing money and to demand more from their financial institutions.

DIVERSIFIED FINANCIAL INSTITUTIONS LAUNDRY LIST OF PRODUCTS

Supermarket	TR	CB	RE	IN	CM	BR	CC
Sears	X	X	X	X	X	X	X
Merrill Lynch			X	X	X	X	X
Prudential			X	X	X	X	X
American Express	X		X	X	X	X	X
American Can		X		X			
Dreyfus		X		X	X	X	
Travelers		X	X	X	X	X	X
Aetna		X	X	X	X	X	
TransAmerica	X	X	X	X		X	
J. C. Penney		X	X	X	X		
John Hancock				X	X	X	

Legend:

TR—Travel-related services
CB—Consumer banking
RE—Real estate sales
IN—Insurance
CM—Cash management
BR—Brokerage
CC—Credit cards

These changing consumer attitudes sent shock waves through the financial community, which had become accustomed to using customers' funds at very attractive rates. Strategic planners within the industry began to focus on how to increase, or even maintain, their market share without unduly sacrificing profit margins. The winners would be those companies that could offer a more complete financial management package for the consumer and sell it efficiently at an attractive price. Merrill Lynch became the leader in product development when, in 1977, it introduced the CMA (cash management account), which combined a number of services traditionally provided separately through a brokerage firm and a commercial bank. For an annual fee, the CMA offered brokerage services, a checking account, a Visa card, automatic investment of idle funds at money market rates, and an optional line of credit. Other institutions followed Merrill Lynch's lead, and competition for customers became fierce. Marketing was the name of the game, and the potential customer base had expanded to include not only high-net-worth individuals but also middle-income Americans who had become more financially savvy and more demanding.

With the increasing popularity of 800 telephone numbers and advanced communications methods, geographic considerations ceased being a major factor in the consumer's decision about which broker to use for stock transactions or which cash management product to purchase. For a company like Sears, technological advances proved advantageous. With the purchase of Dean Witter and Allstate, for example, Sears can now provide brokerage and insurance products at the same location at which a consumer might be shopping for a Roto-tiller.

Eventually, many strategists concluded that the road to success lay in being able to provide so-called womb-to-tomb financial services. It is generally believed that the first "money" product purchased during a person's lifetime is a savings account or checking account, followed by credit cards, car or real estate loans, insurance, and brokerage services. If a firm can capture the consumer early on in this cycle, the chances are good that he or she will remain faithful to the institution.

Banks, insurance companies, and brokerage houses, therefore, have all begun buying into each other's industries in the
hopes of maintaining both market share and profit margins—
a phenomenon referred to as "getting into each other's back-
yard."

The theory behind mergers and acquisitions is that the
newly formed whole will be worth more than just the sum of
its parts. To use the current buzzword, this is the phenomenon of synergy. Financial supermarkets are considered by
some to be highly synergistic. And they have two main advan-
tages: enhanced product development and product sales. Prudential, for example, can take advantage of Pru-Bache's
expertise as brokers to develop new products for its insurance
customers. Conversely, Pru-Bache can call on Prudential to
help develop new real estate, oil and gas, and tax shelter products for sale to Bache's traditional brokerage customers.

One major difficulty facing these financial conglomerates is
developing a unified management style. Because there are
vast differences between management practices at brokerage
firms, insurance companies, commercial banks, and retailers,
organizing these disparate operations into a cohesive whole,
without adversely affecting the productivity of each, is an ongoing concern. Good communication among different operations of the same company is vital to the success of the entire
venture. Strong and effective management can ensure that
companywide policy is filtered down through each of the subsidiaries or divisions, thereby avoiding the pitfalls of a corporate Babel.

A second problem facing the industry is reaching a greater
number of potential customers across the country. Because of
the extensive marketing costs associated with developing a
new product, the campaign must reach a wide enough audi-
ence to justify the expense. One solution many supermarkets
are employing is the acquisition of regional firms. American
Express, for example, purchased Investors Diversified Service, a Minneapolis-based purveyor of mutual funds, life insurance, tax shelters, and other investment products to
Middle America. The acquisition will give American Express
a foothold in the Midwestern market, and help it establish a

national name beyond travel-related products. In the future, successful regional financial services companies will continue to be very attractive takeover targets for larger firms looking to diversify.

JOB OPPORTUNITIES

Because the financial supermarkets are new and growing, they offer many entry-level opportunities, particularly in sales and marketing positions. The availability of jobs, however, is often in direct relation to activity in the financial markets. During bull markets, these firms hire like mad. In 1983, for instance, American Express developed a training program designed to turn out 500 brokers. Sears ran 2,000 trainees through its Dean Witter program during 1983 as well. In 1984, however, many firms were laying off people because the stock market was falling and business dropped off significantly. Because of the increasingly competitive nature of this industry, companies will be looking to gear up the toughest, most aggressive and committed salesforce ever. As conglomerates of sometimes very different operations, these companies run a number of internal training programs. Each division or subsidiary will have its own requirements and its own distinct "corporate culture." In addition to the broad descriptions of training programs in each company described below, it might be helpful to turn to other sections of the book for further information on specific divisions.

**American Express
Company**
American Express Plaza
New York, New York 10004
(212) 323-2000

**Shearson/Lehman/
American Express**
Two World Trade Center
New York, New York 10048
(212) 321-6500

**Fireman's Fund Insurance
Companies**
777 San Marin Drive
Novato, California 94998
(415) 899-2000

The American Express Company is widely diversified, with interests in travel-related services, international banking, insurance, brokerage, and investment banking, to name a few. The company also has a 50 percent interest in Warner Amex, which is involved in the cable TV business. Their most recent acquisition in 1984 was Lehman Brothers, a premier Wall Street firm. They bought the company to enhance their image in corporate finance. Because hiring and training plans were still uncertain at the time of this writing, we have discussed Lehman Brothers separately. American Express is a decentralized organization and each division is run autonomously.

American Express travel-related services manages American Express cards and traveler's checks. It serves the individuals who use the products, the service establishments that accept them, and the financial institutions that distribute them. This division offers a special graduate management program for MBAs. It takes about 60 people a year, 30 of whom are incoming MBAs and the other 30 existing managers in the company. This is more an orientation and networking program than it is straight training. Everyone is hired for a specific job, usually in one of four divisions: finance and planning, marketing and sales, systems and data processing, and operations. The program begins in the fall and runs until the following summer. The main purpose of the program, according to one graduate, is to develop management skills and to "network" within the organization by gaining exposure to the different operating units of the company. Senior managers address the program participants in a series of seminars, and workshops are held in time management, public speaking, and project management. In addition, all new hires go on a few sales calls, even if they are not slated for this division. Business overview case studies are done in small groups and then presented to a senior executive of the company.

On its own, Shearson/Lehman/American Express is one of the major securities firms in the United States. It is the fourth largest in terms of registered representatives and the third largest in terms of equity capital, and it ranks highly in underwriting. This division offers two entry-level tracks for MBAs. Each year it hires five or six associates to take part in a general management training program. After orientation to the firm, new hires work on different projects lasting from three to sixteen weeks each. These assignments expose them to different areas of the company, including retail branches, operations, treasury, marketing, and capital markets (trading). At the end of the year-long program, associates are placed in an area where they have expressed an interest and where the firm has a need.

The other option is for MBAs to come in as associates in either corporate or public finance. The majority of new associates spend their first two years as part of an associate pool in which they are expected to develop generalist investment banking skills. There is no structured training, but associates have the opportunity to work in a number of different areas, including syndicate and over-the-counter trading.

For BAs and BSs, Shearson also offers a management development program in securities operations and capital markets (trading). There is also a data processing training program that leads to a position as senior programmer or senior analyst.

Fireman's Fund Insurance is a collection of property, liability, and life insurance companies with offices throughout the United States and Canada. Fireman's Fund does not work directly with the public; rather it conducts business solely through agents and brokers. The company considers itself to be one of the leading insurers of the entertainment industry, writing policies for film and television productions. Insurance opportunities are offered in a variety of areas, including underwriting, sales, actuarial science, claims, loss control, finance, and systems.

American Express also offers a special training program at the corporate level for those with undergraduate degrees in business, accounting, economics, or other quantitative subjects. This financial management program involves two years of rotations complemented by formal classroom training. Each work assignment lasts six months and may be in accounting and control, financial reports and analysis, treasury, or tax. Courses are also given in finance, accounting, planning, management informations systems, general management, marketing, and interpersonal skills. Permanent assignments are determined after two years on the basis of performance and personal goals. It is possible to move into one of the operating companies at the conclusion of training.

Salaries for MBAs joining the travel-related program are between $30,000 and $35,000. The exact figure depends on prior work experience. The firm would not disclose salary information for the other areas. Benefits include major medical and dental coverage, insurance, reduced minimums on money market funds, and reduced commissions on stock transactions.

**Prudential Insurance
Company of America
Prudential Plaza
Newark, New Jersey 07101
(201) 877-8000**

**Prudential-Bache Securities
100 Gold Street
New York, New York 10292
(212) 791-1000**

**Prucapital
153 Halsey Street
Prudential Plaza
Newark, New Jersey 07101
(201) 877-6000**

Prudential is the largest insurance company in the world. It is also an incredibly diverse company, with operations not only in the insurance business but also in securities, investment banking, real estate, and business lending.

Prudential's investment operations group offers a number of entry-level opportunities. Its goal is to maximize the return that Prudential makes on its portfolio of premium payments. The group consists of capital markets, real estate investment, asset management, and PRUCAPITAL.

Approximately five MBAs are hired as analysts into the capital markets group each year. The three-month training period is 75 percent casework and 25 percent seminars. Courses on loan agreements, oil and gas partnerships, finance companies, and leverage buyouts are taught by in-house personnel. New analysts learn to evaluate various deals in which Prudential may become an investor. The analysts help determine whether the deals are structured appropriately and whether they will provide an adequate return. After the three-month training period, analysts are assigned to either corporate finance, which handles private placements, or public bond and money markets, which invests in both taxable and tax-exempt public securities. During the first few years with the company, analysts have the opportunity to transfer between these two divisions and to rotate among the various management teams.

PRUCAPITAL has job opportunities for about ten MBAs per year. PRUCAPITAL provides short- and intermediate-term financing, leases, revolving lines of credit, and leveraged buyout equity and debt investments to middle-market customers and to firms in the bottom portion of the Fortune 500 list. Analysts help develop new investment opportunities through their marketing efforts, analyze credit, evaluate risks, structure deals and negotiate them, and coordinate with the other areas of the institution to ensure good delivery.

Prudential-Bache is the securities arm of Prudential. It was formed in 1981, when Prudential bought Bache Halsey Stuart & Shields. Pru-Bache is trying to establish itself as one of the leading investment banks on The Street. The investment banking arm of Pru-Bache hires around thirteen BA analysts a year to work in a generalist pool. Analysts are expected to go to business school after their two-year assignment. Training consists of in-house presentations on technical procedures used in the firm. Over the course of their stay, analysts may receive assignments in a number of areas, including energy, financial institutions, industrials, information industries, transportation and leasing, capital banking, and private placements.

Approximately six to twelve MBAs are hired at the entry level as associates each year. They too are expected to work as generalists, and their training begins with a seven-week orientation program in which they learn about the firm's different divisions and subsequently rotate through them. During this period, associates are expected to take the registered representative (Series Seven) exam. After orientation, associates enter a pool and are assigned to a number of teams in different areas of the investment banking division. After one to three years, depending on background, performance, and the firm's needs, associates are assigned to specific industry or functional groups.

Salaries vary across the country. Generally, Prudential's investment division associates start in the mid-thirties, as do PRUCAPITAL associates. Pru-Bache analysts get $26,000 and associates make over $40,000. Benefits include major medical coverage, life insurance, profit sharing (bonus), reduced commissions on stock transactions, and tuition reimbursement.

8/
Insurance Companies

Insurance, like commercial banking, used to be a relatively straightforward business. Insurers collected premiums on policies, invested them at a steady rate of return, paid out a reasonable amount of their income in claims, and reinvested the surplus for the firm. Over the years, changes in the insurance business have mirrored the evolution of the financial services industry as a whole. In periods of volatile interest rates, investment income has become more difficult to predict, and diversification has become the name of the game. Today, a number of insurance companies are involved in a wide range of outside activities—from managing pension funds for other companies to owning car rental agencies.

TYPES OF INSURERS

There are basically three types of insurance companies: life insurance, property* and casualty,* and reinsurance.* Whereas life insurance companies write policies covering—you guessed it—life, property and casualty companies insure against property damage and bodily injury. Reinsurers buy participations in particularly large policies for which the "primary" company is unwilling or unable to accept all the risk. Recently the large insurance companies have begun to provide all three of these services because, they believe, synergies will be created that will enable them to sell the various insurance products more efficiently.

Most property and casualty insurers are organized as mutual insurance companies. Mutuals are owned by the policyholders. Stock companies, in contrast, are publicly held corporations designed to earn a profit for shareholders. According to industry analysts, the property and casualty business is in the midst of a shakeout. In 1982 and 1983, for example, an unusually large number of claims arising from natural disasters and lower prices on policies arising from increased competition forced the industry to pay out $23 billion more in claims that it collected in premiums. These problems have been compounded by a drop-off in corporate business as large companies began insuring themselves through captive insurance* subsidiaries.

The life insurance industry has also been having its share of difficulties. Although cash flow from investments has been bolstered by high yields and a strong stock market, new policies have fallen considerably. It seems that during recessionary periods life insurance becomes a luxury. In addition, many companies permit their customers to take out loans against their policies. In this situation, premiums stop coming in, and the insurance company is forced to lend money out, usually at a concessionary rate of interest.

ORGANIZATION

Insurers are divided along functional lines into three distinct areas: underwriting and technical support, sales, and investment.

Underwriting

Underwriting is the "meat and potatoes" of the insurance industry. Underwriters determine the risks an insurance company should take and calculate the premiums necessary to provide an adequate return in light of the risk taken. This profession requires strong analytical skills and sound judgment. Even when the numbers in a deal look good, underwriters may decide not to issue a policy, or price it out of the market, because it doesn't "feel" right.

Underwriters are supported in this decision-making process by a corps of engineers and actuaries. Insurance engineers are data collectors in the property and casualty business. (Doctors fulfill this function in underwriting life insurance policies.) Their job is to determine the condition of a plant or a piece of property or equipment to be insured. Engineers inspect the premises and look at the electrical wiring, construction quality, and other structural elements. All these factors will affect the underwriter's decision and pricing strategy. Engineers are also responsible for visiting clients on an ongoing basis and suggesting methods for improving safety and reducing the chances of damage.

Actuaries work closely with underwriters, providing them with the quantitative analyses needed to evaluate specific risks. Actuarial science is a highly technical field that emphasizes the use of computer models to predict the probability of events (such as deaths or drunk driving accidents) on the basis of historical precedents. Only with this information can insurers be reasonably certain of covering their risks by charging adequate premiums or by selling part of their policy to a reinsurer.

An insurance company doesn't only sell insurance, it must also ensure that the terms of its policies are being met and that any claims are justifiable. This function is performed by premium auditors and claim-and-loss representatives. Premium auditors work at client firms auditing accounting information to ensure that the terms of their policies are being followed. Premiums are often adjusted upward or downward as a result of these audits. Claim-and-loss representatives are the insurance companies' front line. Whenever a claim is made, they're the ones who evaluate the damage and estimate the cost of repair or settlement. These claims can range from a "fender bender" incident to a car rental agency destroyed by a tornado. The representatives must determine whether the company should pay a claim and, if so, how much.

Sales

Insurance distribution employs over a third of the professionals in the industry. Agents are certified by the American
Agency System, a nationwide network of insurance agents, or
sales representatives. They are the retail point of contact and
often represent a number of insurers for different products,
such as car, home, and life insurance. Agents spend most of
their time developing business, prospecting, and trying to sell
policies, but they also act as liaisons between their customers
and their insurers. Agents are self-employed and receive commissions on the policies they sell. As a result, they need to be
aggressive in seeking out new business.

Many large insurers now have their own branch offices,
which sell their policies directly to retail clients. This helps
reduce selling costs, since agents in the branch offices are paid
a salary instead of on a commission basis.

Independent insurance brokers act as intermediaries between their clients—large institutional customers—and the
insurance companies. Brokers usually serve as consultants, researching their clients' needs and trying to match them with
the most appropriate type of policy. They then approach the
insurance companies and work out the details of a policy.
Brokers also recommend methods of reducing their clients'
premium expenses, perhaps by improving in-house safety
standards and modifying or replacing equipment.

Reinsurance is a worldwide system of sharing risk. In many
ways, it is analogous to a loan or underwriting syndication,
when a lender or investor either cannot or chooses not to
accept the risk of an entire undertaking. In the insurance
business, the reinsurer is paid a premium by the original in-
surer according to the portion of the risk that is assumed.
Risks are assumed on either a pro rata or a surplus share basis.
In a pro rata plan the risks are shared proportionately,
whereas in a surplus share plan reinsurers accept the risk for
claims exceeding an agreed-upon amount. Reinsurance is particularly important today, when hundred-million-dollar risks
are underwritten in the property and casualty field regularly.
After all, who would want to assume all the risks associated
with a nuclear power plant?

Investment

After successfully underwriting and selling policies, insurance companies need to invest the premiums they collect. When economic conditions are stable, this is a relatively simple task. As the investment environment has become more volatile, however, insurance companies have had to devise increasingly sophisticated methods for investing their funds.

Insurance companies invest in three major areas: capital markets, securities, and real estate. In the capital markets, they serve as long-term lenders through private placements. Companies that want to raise long-term funds but that do not have access to the public markets, usually because of their creditworthiness, find willing investors in the insurance companies, which are happy to lock up their money for long periods of time if the return is right. The responsibilities of the capital markets group include evaluating specific projects and determining whether they meet the company's investment criteria.

Insurance companies are also the largest institutional investors in the securities market. Because prices are so volatile today, large staffs of investment professionals oversee the disposition of funds in short-term money market instruments, bonds, and equities. Some companies—for instance, Prudential—can have over $100 million in cash to invest on any given day. Because of their expertise in the investment area, a number of the larger insurers also manage assets for other companies' pension funds.

Real estate is an area in which insurers have traditionally invested heavily. They participate in deals either as lenders or as investors. The insurance companies generally work on very large real estate projects—shopping centers, housing developments, and office buildings, to name a few.

JOB OPPORTUNITIES

Insurance companies offer a number of career opportunities for entry-level hires. BAs with a strong math background can go into actuarial science. When they join a company, they will be expected to sit for the actuarial examinations and eventually become members of the Society of Actuaries. Salaries for this position vary in direct proportion to how many exams the employee has passed. Many insurance companies offer in-house training for these exams or help new hires meet the cost of an outside class.

Sales and premium auditing also offer opportunities for BAs. Both careers entail quite a bit of traveling. Sales can be a very challenging first job. It involves actively seeking out business in a very competitive environment and thus can be either a very frustrating or a very rewarding experience. Suffice it to say that the turnover in this position is extremely high.

MBAs can find interesting job opportunities in the investment area. Insurance companies hire MBAs to evaluate investment options and make recommendations on the company's course of action. These positions usually pay well and offer the opportunity for substantial responsibility and financial creativity.

Aetna Life and Casualty
One Civic Center Plaza
Hartford, Connecticut 06143
(203) 273-0123

Aetna is one of the biggest insurance companies in the United States, marketing all types of business insurance, personal insurance, and pension products. In addition, the company is involved in real estate and high-technology investment. The company operates offices all over the United States as well as overseas.

Aetna offers opportunities for MBAs who are interested in analyst positions in the bond investment department or the real estate department. The firm hires five to ten MBAs per year to take part in this program. The bond investment department is responsible for managing the company's investments in all fixed-income securities, both taxable and tax-exempt. Analysts spend some time in credit analysis, where they analyze bond issues, negotiate terms, and get involved in marketing. In this capacity, they probably spend upwards of 25 percent of their time on the road. Analysts also do a stint in portfolio management, where they work on investment strategies and choose various types of investments that they think will yield a good return for the company. They also spend time in investment research, where they develop new investment products and/or techniques.

The real estate investment department manages Aetna's real estate investments. As analysts in this section, new hires review and analyze mortgage loan offerings and negotiate terms. They are responsible for making recommendations to the company about the suitability of various real estate investments.

Salaries for MBAs start in the low to mid-thirties. Benefits include major medical and dental coverage, reduced insurance rates, and a savings incentive plan.

CIGNA
Hartford, Connecticut 06152
(203) 726-6000

CIGNA was formed in 1982 when Connecticut General, a group health, life, and employee benefits company, merged with INA, a major player in the property and casualty business. CIGNA is now one of the largest financial services organizations in the United States.

CIGNA has recently developed a training program for its individual financial division (IFD) counselors. IFD is a part of the company's employee benefits and financial services group. IFD markets a broad array of financial services—including tax planning, investment planning, fringe benefit planning, business consulting, and estate planning—to small business owners, senior corporate executives, and other professionals. Counselors draw on the array of products and services offered by CIGNA and market them to their customers.

The company hires individuals with backgrounds in accounting, personal taxation, investment planning, or small business counseling and two years of work experience. Trainees begin their career in one of CIGNA's nationwide field offices. After training, those with MBAs go to another field location or to Philadelphia or Hartford, where the company's two main headquarters are located.

The first phase of the management training program focuses on learning about the products offered by the company and building selling skills. Trainees must demonstrate competence in these areas before they are permitted to take on account management responsibility. In the second phase of the program, trainees are permitted to manage client relationships on their own.

The company would not disclose salary and benefits information.

Equitable Life Assurance Society of the United States
1285 Avenue of the Americas
New York, New York 10019
(212) 554-1234

Equitable offers a management development program for MBAs in its pension department. The pension area manages and administers more than $30 billion in pension and thrift plan assets. Clients include Fortune 500 companies as well as smaller regional clients. The goals of the program are to teach trainees the pension business, the analytical techniques used in the industry, and Equitable's marketing and investment strategies. The program is also used as a means of identifying fast-trackers in the organization.

Training consists of a series of rotations that last from 18 to 24 months. Trainees spend time in marketing, where they develop market research and study the competition. They also do a stint in account management, working with senior account executives on specific relationships and assisting in the marketing of pension investment products to established and new customers. Later they spend time in business development and strategic planning, developing and analyzing financial and business plans. Finally, trainees work in product development, where they contribute to the design of new products and make recommendations on pricing strategies.

During the rotational period, trainees have the opportunity to meet with senior management, attending monthly meetings with the head of the pension department to discuss business developments and other topics of interest. Equitable evaluates trainees at the conclusion of each rotational assignment. Final placement is determined by individual preference and the needs of the organization.

Salaries for MBAs start in the low to mid-thirties. Benefits include major medical coverage and discounts on insurance premiums.

General Reinsurance Corporation
600 Steamboat Road
Greenwich, Connecticut 06830
(203) 644-4000

General Reinsurance is one of the largest and most successful reinsurers in the United States. Headquartered in Greenwich, the company also offers training at its New York City facilities.

GenRe hires approximately ten trainees a year for both property underwriting and casualty underwriting. Most trainees are BAs; some MBAs are hired for the financial risk department, which insures against loss in financial deals. Training consists of courses held at the College of Insurance in downtown Manhattan, a series of case studies, and in-house lectures given by senior members of the corporation, all supplemented by on-the-job experience. The courses given at the College of Insurance include principles of insurance, property insurance, casualty insurance, and property loss control. Trainees are also required to write a twenty-page term paper on a topic of their choice. All trainees are guaranteed a position when they complete the program. After two or three years, they are promoted to assistant secretary.

Starting salaries range from $15,000 to $20,000 for BAs. Benefits include medical and dental coverage, life insurance, profit sharing, pension plan, credit cards, tuition reimbursement, a complete set of luggage, and a briefcase.

Mutual Life Insurance Company of New York (MONY)
1740 Broadway
New York, New York 10019
(212) 708-2000

MONY was one of the first insurance companies to sell insurance to the general public *and,* it claims, the first to sell insurance to women. MONY is headquartered in New York, with an operations center in Syracuse and over 200 field and service offices in major cities throughout the United States.

The company offers career development programs in a variety of areas, including finance and accounting, group products, human resources, investment departments, office operations, actuarial science, group and pension sales, electronic data processing, and life insurance sales. Career development is a combination of on-the-job experience and specialized training in professional skills. All new hires take part in the corporate orientation program, which is designed to develop knowledge of the insurance business in general and MONY in particular. Training and development seminars are also given in time management, oral presentations, career planning, and management skills.

Liberal arts graduates with no technical background may find opportunities in a number of areas, including the controller's department (where they work on corporate budgeting, productivity, and cost reduction), human resources, and office operations. Undergraduates with a major in business or accounting are hired into the corporate finance department, which handles tax, accounting, and planning issues. Those with a strong background in math or accounting are hired into the group insurance department, which services employee benefits programs of small and multinational businesses, and into the group pension department, which manages the company's portfolio of pension funds. Individuals with both coursework and job experience in the securities industry may be interested in joining the securities investment department, which is responsible for all fixed-income investments, including preferred stocks and bonds. The real estate and mortgage investment division hires entry-level candidates

208

with an accounting, business administration, or real estate background.

Individuals with a strong math background can join MONY's actuarial program, which is designed to prepare new hires to take the exams given semiannually by the Society of Actuaries. The firm provides anywhere from 100 to 150 hours of study time, depending on which level of examination the actuary is taking. At the same time trainees are given rotational assignments in three or four areas, including individual insurance, group insurance, group pensions, and corporate finance. Assignments last about one year each and increase in responsibility as more and more of the actuarial exams are passed. When employees become fellows of the Society of Actuaries, a process that usually takes years, they also become officers of the company.

Group and pension sales also has a formalized training program for new hires, which begins with three months in the home office learning the basics of group life and health insurance, corporate pensions, profit sharing, and thrift plans. Subsequently, trainees are sent out to one of the field offices, where they learn how to conduct meetings with prospective clients. After these two phases are completed, trainees are promoted to group and pension sales representatives. At this time, they are encouraged to take outside seminars and advanced courses given by professional industry associations.

Life insurance sales puts college grads through a training program that covers the fundamentals of insurance as well as advanced topics in life insurance marketing, financial counseling, estate planning, and business insurance.

MONY also offers an office supervisor training program designed to train individuals to take on the responsibilites of sales agency office supervisors. The program combines on-the-job training and case studies to teach new hires the basics of insurance, MONY's products and procedures, personnel policies, and office management skills. New hires spend eight to twelve months in one of the agencies and are evaluated by a trainer from the home office in New York who makes periodic visits to the agencies. Trainees may be asked to move from agency to agency during this time; they also attend seminars at the service center in Syracuse and at headquarters. At the conclusion of the program, participants are promoted to office supervisors.

Salaries range from $18,000 to $32,000. Benefits include medical coverage, life insurance, flexible work hours, investment plan, and tuition refund program.

Penn Mutual Life Insurance Company
Independence Square
Philadelphia, Pennsylvania 19172
(215) 629-0600

Penn Mutual markets life and health insurance, pensions, annuities, and profit-sharing plans. It offers entry-level training programs in its actuarial, auditing, controller, marketing, pension, sales, and underwriting departments. In all, Penn Mutual hires approximately 30 college graduates per year. Penn Mutual hires entry-level actuaries, who do statistical work analyzing data on death, disability, and injury—the very events that insurance companies are insuring against. The higher the expected probability of an event, the higher the insurance premium will be. Actuaries at Penn Mutual must pass two exams, and the company allows them a minimum of 100 hours to spend on the job in study time.

The company also hires entry-level underwriters each year. Underwriters determine whether a prospective individual or corporate policyholder is acceptable and what premium the policyholder should be paying. Penn Mutual provides formalized classroom training to prepare underwriters for the required certification exam.

Training for other divisions takes place mostly on the job, with some supplemental seminars offered to those in the auditing and pension departments.

Penn Mutual would not disclose salary information. Benefits include medical insurance, free lunch program, 100 percent tuition reimbursement, flexible work hours, auto insurance at special rates, and incentive savings program.

Royal Insurance
150 William Street
New York, New York 10038
(212) 553-3000

Royal Insurance is headquartered in New York, with territorial offices in Boston, Chicago, Philadelphia, and Syracuse. The company does business in all fifty states. Royal offers entry-level national training in four job categories: marketing representative, underwriter, claim-and-loss representative, and premium auditor.

Marketing representatives sell Royal's insurance product line to sales agents and insurance brokers. It is up to them to develop strategies to place as many Royal services in the hands of the individual sales representative as possible. Training for this job consists of a nine-month session, approximately a third of which is spent in class. Courses in product presentations, sales skills, and premium pricing are taught by in-house personnel. An overview of the insurance industry is also provided. After each class segment, which lasts about two weeks, trainees work on projects and provide some backup support for established marketing officers. After nine months, they are assigned to work with a marketing officer, planning strategies and going on calls. When trainees are judged ready to go out on their own, they are given independent responsibility for a particular geographic region.

Royal Insurance does have entry-level underwriter positions. Their training is fairly unstructured and consists of a number of presentations made in casualty, fidelity and burglary, inland marine, marine, personal, property, and boiler and machinery insurance. Training is designed so that in-class presentations complement what the underwriter is doing on the job. Trainees also go on field trips with practicing underwriters to gain familiarity with live client situations. It takes approximately one year to become a practicing underwriter.

Claim-and-loss representative positions are open to BAs and BSs. Training is provided in damage appraisal methods and claims processing policies. Trainees spend four weeks at the Vale National Institute in Pennsylvania learning automobile and building appraisal methodologies. Further in-house training is offered in how to interpret and explain insurance policies to policyholders. The length of time until representatives begin working independently is based solely on individual progress.

Royal Insurance also hires entry-level actuaries, primarily with math degrees, who are expected to have one or two of the actuarial exams behind them when they join the company. The on-the-job exposure they receive is designed to help prepare them for specific actuarial exams.

The company would not disclose salary information. Benefits include cut-rate insurance, tuition reimbursement, employee savings plan, and profit sharing.

Sentry Insurance
1800 North Point Drive
Stevens Point, Wisconsin 54481
(715) 346-6000

Sentry was originally founded in 1904 as Hardware Mutual and currently has interests in insurance, radio and cable TV, manufacturing, oil and gas exploration, financial services, and automobile leasing. The insurance company provides life and health disability insurance, as well as property and casualty coverage. The company is actually an amalgamation of five different insurance firms. Sentry operates out of four major locations: Stevens Point, Wisconsin (headquarters); Scottsdale, Arizona; Atlanta, Georgia; and Concord, Massachusetts.

Sentry offers entry-level opportunities for underwriters, sales representatives, claims representatives, marketing officers, accountants, actuaries, and data processors.

Underwriters are trained through project work as well as through outside courses for which Sentry picks up the tab. The courses are designed to prepare candidates to pass the certification exam for property and casualty or life insurance underwriters. Actuaries must also pass exams, and the firm provides study time for this purpose.

Sales representatives go through thirteen weeks of instruction, which introduces them to the company's line of products. Sentry also has a nine-week on-the-job program in data processing designed to teach even the uninitiated about programming techniques and Sentry's computer systems.

The firm would not disclose salary information. Benefits include group health and life insurance, disability insurance, investment plan, flexible work hours, credit union, tuition reimbursement for business degree programs or short-term courses, and an on-premises gymnasium.

References

INDUSTRY-RELATED REFERENCE BOOKS

Accounting

The Big Eight: An Insider's View of America's Eight Most Powerful and Influential Accounting Firms by Mark Stevens (Macmillan, 1981)
An in-depth look at the Big Eight. A colorful work, the book presents a behind-the-scenes side of accounting that may be a surprise to prospective applicants.

Banking

The Bankers by Martin Mayer (Ballantine Books, 1974)
A classic description of the banking world and the changing regulatory environment in which it operates.

Commercial Banking in the Economy by Paul Nadler (Random House, 1979)
An examination of the role played by the banking industry as it affects credit control and economic activity.

The Money Lenders by Anthony Sampson (Viking Press, 1982)
A description of the activities of the international financial world and how individual personalities in the banking com-

munity have affected the global economy. Particular focus is placed on Morgan Guaranty, Citibank, Chase Manhattan, and Bank of America.

Economics

The Complete Bond Book by David Darst (McGraw-Hill, 1975)
Good, understandable description of trading instruments and how they work. A great book to read if you're going for a job in sales and trading. David Darst has been affiliated with Goldman Sachs.

Economics Explained by Robert Heilbroner and Lester Thurow (Prentice-Hall, 1982)
A thoroughly understandable book on modern economics. Contains an excellent appendix on how the banking system works. Very good for interview preparation.

Interest Rate Futures by Alan M. Loosigian. (Dow Jones–Irwin, 1980).

The Money Market: Myth, Reality, and Practice by Marcia Stigum (Dow Jones–Irwin, 1978)

INFORMATION FOR COMPILING COMPANY FILES

Directories

AICPA Annual Surveys
Annual surveys of the accounting profession. Available from the American Institute of Certified Public Accountants (AICPA), Public Relations Department, 1211 Avenue of the Americas, New York, NY 10036.

American Economic and Business History: A Guide to Information Sources by Robert W. Lovett, (Gale, 1971)
A bibliography listing published histories of particular companies. Very useful for interviewing files. If a book has been written about a prospective employer, you should at least know the title!

Best's Insurance Reports
The most comprehensive reports on insurance companies available.

Million-Dollar Directory
Published by Dun & Bradstreet. Lists over 120,000 corporations, their primary officers, number of employees, addresses, products, and other information.

Standard and Poor's Register of Corporations, Directors, and Executives
Similar to *Million-Dollar Directory*.

Periodicals

Accounting News, quarterly
American Banker, daily
Barron's, weekly
Business Week, weekly
Forbes, bi-weekly
Fortune, bi-weekly
Institutional Investor, monthly
The New York Times, daily
The Wall Street Journal, daily

Periodicals Indexes

Predicast's F&S Index United States
Lists articles written on specific industries and companies that have appeared in a number of financial and business publications. Published weekly.

Wall Street Journal Index
A monthly compilation of all articles appearing in the *Wall Street Journal.* Broken down into corporate news and general news.

Reports

Annual Reports
Issued annually by publicly held companies. Contains discussion of lines of business as well as financial results.

216

Value Line Reports
Investor-oriented reports, updated four times a year, on over
1,500 companies, including those in the financial services industry.

JOB-HUNTING AIDS

The College Graduate's Career Guide by Robert J. Ginn, Jr.
(Scribner's, 1981)
A very broad work, ranging from self-assessment and career
exploration to specific job-hunting techniques. Includes a substantial reference section.

Directory of College Recruiting Personnel
Published by the College Placement Council, Bethlehem,
Pennsylvania.

Dress for Success by John T. Molloy (Warner Books, 1975)
Power clothes.

The Employer's Guide to Interviewing by Robert L. Genua (Prentice-Hall, 1979)
A book for interviewers that describes the various screening
stages and offers suggested questions for eliciting specific information from candidates. The better you know how interviewers operate, the better your chances of feeling more
comfortable yourself.

How to Pass the Employment Interview (with Flying Colors) by W.
G. Ryckman (Dow Jones–Irwin, 1982)
Predominantly aimed at undergraduates, this guide contains
hints for on-campus recruiting and how to prepare for interviews. The book lists a series of typical questions and answers
from actual interviews and presents a series of suggested follow-up steps to the interview.

How to Turn an Interview into a Job by Jeffrey G. Allen (Simon
& Schuster, 1983)
Concentrates on what applicants need to convey during the
limited time allowed in an interview along with a number of
interviewing strategies designed to help applicants be aggressive without seeming pushy. It is a good primer for those who
have a difficult time selling themselves.

217

Occupational Outlook Handbook
Published by the U.S. Department of Labor, Bureau of Labor
Statistics, Washington, D.C.

The Professional Job Search Program by Burton E. Lipman.
(Wiley-Interscience, 1983)
Another step-by-step guide that concentrates on sample cover
letters and résumés. The author also includes strategies for
"test mailings" and salary negotiations.

What Color Is Your Parachute? by Richard Nelson Bolles (Ten
Speed Press, 1983)
A very popular general career guide updated annually. The
book starts with the career decision and follows with a step-
by-step description of the job search, suggesting a series of
specific action steps to help you find a job in the field of your
choice.

The Woman's Dress for Success Book by John T. Molloy (Follett
Publishing Company, 1977)
Power clothes for women.

Glossary

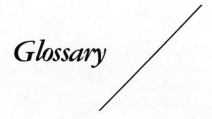

account executive (AE)   The person who manages accounts at retail brokerage and insurance firms.

account officer (AO)   A bank officer who has direct *line* responsibility for a particular account or client corporation. Also called a relationship manager, line officer, lending officer, or *platform officer.*

arbitrage (arb)   Purchasing and selling securities simultaneously and making a profit through price differentials. Arbitrageurs, or arbs, take advantage of market inefficiencies—that is, when prices of the same instrument should logically be the same but are different in different markets.

asset-based financing   Lending money, usually to a small company, by securing the debt to the company's assets. For example, ABC Bank lends Acme Manufacturing $2 million and holds as *collateral* Acme's $2 million warehouse. Most lending to *Fortune 500* companies is unsecured—that is, there is no collateral pledged.

ATM   Automated teller machine. A computerized machine that automatically performs cash and other banking transactions by insertion of a banking card. ATMs are gradually replacing tellers at many banks.

bank holding company   A corporation that owns or controls one or more banks but really exists only on paper. Holding companies initially permitted banks to get around state laws limiting interstate banking. Now holding companies allow banks to expand into other activities such as discount brokerage and leasing.

Bear Market　When there are more sellers than buyers in a financial market.

Best's Insurance Reports　The foremost source of information on the insurance industry. These annuals include an analysis of each company's operations.

Big Board　The New York Stock Exchange.

bond　A certificate issued by companies to raise money. The issuer promises to pay the holder the entire amount plus interest according to an agreed-upon schedule.

booking　Booking a loan. A common term for getting business in commercial banking.

Bull Market　Opposite of a bear market. Bull markets make brokerage firms very happy.

calls　In banking, a visit paid on a client corporation. In some bank training programs, trainees begin going out on calls immediately; in others, they slowly work up to making calls. In brokerage, a call refers to a telephone call made to clients and/or prospects. In the futures market, a call is an *option* to buy a security at a specified price at a specified time in the future. See also *cold call.*

capital markets　The markets where *equity* and long-term debt are issued and traded.

captive insurance company　An insurance company owned by a corporation to insure risk inherent in its business.

cash flow underwriting　In insurance, remaining profitable by virtue of obtaining income from investments even though the company's insurance operations are losing money.

casualty　Insurance offered as protection against bodily injury.

CBOE　Chicago Board of Options Exchange, the largest market for *options* in the United States.

CDs　Certificates of deposit. Instruments issued by commercial banks in order to raise deposits. Invented by Walter Wriston of Citibank, CDs carry a specified rate of interest, which may or may not be regulated by the Federal Reserve Board.

cold call   A first meeting with a prospective customer.

collateral   Property, securities, or cash given to a lender to secure an obligation.

COMEX   New York Commodities Exchange. Commodities contracts are traded either in the spot market (for delivery in two days) or in the forward market (for delivery in the future at a previously agreed-upon price). COMEX is second only to the Chicago Board of Trade in contract volume.

commercial paper   Short-term corporate IOUs. Commercial paper is issued by major corporations whose creditworthiness is not really in doubt. It is a very cheap source of funds because the company has direct access to the *money markets* rather than having to go through a bank.

commodities   Readily marketable staples such as pork bellies, beef, grains, or oil.

commodities contract   A contract to buy or sell commodities at an agreed-upon date at an agreed-upon price.

corbanking   Correspondent banking. In commercial banking, maintaining accounts with other banks—correspondents—in order to facilitate financial transactions. Corbank officers are the relationship managers for other commercial banks.

CPA   Certified public accountant. Most accounting firms require that their employees become CPAs by passing the certification exam.

cross   To match a buy order with a sell order. A sales and trading term.

deficit   The federal budget deficit. Often considered a significant contributor to interest rate movments.

ding letters   Rejection letters.

divestiture   When a company sells one of its divisions or subsidiaries.

D&B   Dun & Bradstreet. One of the most widely followed bond-rating agencies, also the oldest. D&B provides customers with evaluations of the creditworthiness of numer-

221

ous institutions and corporations, even those that are not public companies.

Edge Act Legislation enabling a bank to set up a subsidiary solely to handle international business. Because of their special purpose, Edge Act subsidiaries may be set up outside a bank's home state.

engagement An auditing assignment for an accounting firm, handled by an "engagement team."

equity The owner's investment in a company, evidenced by *stock*.

Eurodollars (Euros) U.S. dollar deposit claims held by banks located outside the United States or an overseas branch of a domestic bank. Although the claims to the funds are overseas, the Eurodollars never actually leave the United States. Because Euros are not subject to Federal Reserve requirements, they are often a cheaper source of funds for corporations that need to borrow money. A Eurodollar loan is a bank loan with a price based upon the Eurodollar rate.

Euromarket Overseas market for financial instruments.

factoring When a bank or factoring company purchases receivables from a corporation at a discount from face value. For example, let's suppose you bought an $80 item on credit from Bloomingdale's. Bloomingdale's would have an $80 receivable. If they were in need of cash, however, they could sell this receivable for less than face value, say $78. This is factoring, and the factoring company would receive $80 at the end of the credit term. The discount charged is similar to the interest rate charged on a typical loan.

Fannie Mae Federal National Mortgage Association. A privately owned corporation that buys mortgages when mortgage financing in banks and savings and loan institutions is tight and then sells them when the supply of loanable dollars is strong. Fannie May finances itself by issuing securities, referred to as Fannie Maes, which are very popular with institutional investors.

Fed The Federal Reserve Board, a committee appointed by the President and charged with regulating credit in the

United States. Its decisions and actions in the open market are considered one of the major influences of interest rate movements.

Fed funds   Deposits of banks at the Federal Reserve. Banks can borrow or lend these funds in the interbank market (that is, among themselves).

fiduciary   An institution to which property is entrusted for someone else's benefit. For example, banks play a fiduciary role through their trust departments by managing investments for others and by acting as trustees on debt and *equity* issues.

Fitch   One of the major bond-rating agencies.

Fortune 500/Fortune 1000   *Fortune* magazine's listing of the largest corporations in America. People often use the term Fortune 500 to describe very large companies. Recently, the listing was divided into the Fortune 500 for industrial companies and the Fortune Service 500 for the service industries, including banking, and insurance.

futures contract   A commitment to buy a specified amount of a commodity or a financial product at a fixed price in the future. Used to protect against future price changes.

FX   Foreign exchange, or currencies of different nations. There are FX traders, FX rooms, FX desks, and so on, in investment and commercial banks.

GAAP   Generally accepted accounting principles. Promulgated by the Financial Accounting Standards Board, GAAPs are the laws that govern accounting practices.

Garn–St. Germain   Legislation effective in 1982 that allows commercial banks to offer interest-bearing checking accounts. Considered revolutionary, it has been a major impetus in changing the way commercial banks do business.

generals   Any *stock* traded on an exchange for over $100 a share.

Glass-Steagall   Legislation passed in 1933 separating the functions of commercial banks from those of investment banks.

Govis   U.S. government securities. Commercial banks and investment banks have "government desks" where these types of financial instruments are exclusively traded.

house An investment bank. The houses on *The Street* refers to the investment banks on Wall Street.

institutional investors A large investor, such as a bank, insurance company, trust, or pension fund.

IPO Initial public offering. Used in investment banking circles to denote the first time a company offers shares for sale in the open market.

junk bonds Bonds of companies that do not receive high ratings from *S&P, D&B, Moody's* or *Fitch* but that yield high returns for investors because of their perceived riskiness.

leverage A numerical measurement used to represent the amount of debt a firm has on its balance sheet relative to the amount of *equity*. Often used as a tool for determining the financial health, and capacity for growth, of an enterprise.

leveraged buyout (LBO) The purchase of a company or a particular subsidiary of a company by management. The assets of the new entity are pledged as *collateral* for the debt required for the purchase.

LIBOR London interbank offered rate. The rate at which London banks trade *Eurodollar* deposits. Basically the same as the Eurodollar rate.

Line of credit/revolver In commercial banking, a fixed amount of borrowed funds that a customer is permitted to have outstanding at any one time. For example, if you have a $1,000 line of credit on your Visa card, you can charge $1,000 worth of goods, pay for them, and then charge $1,000 more. Revolving lines of credit are given to corporations just as they are given to credit card users.

line versus staff A line officer's primary function is to be in direct contact with customers. Staff officers deal almost exclusively with internal situations in support of the line.

long Owning a security. This is the direct opposite of being *short*, a situation in which investors sell securities they don't own in the hope of being able to buy them back more cheaply later. For example, if you believe the price of a particular stock is going to go down, you can put in an order to sell it at today's price, and then buy the stock a week later when the price is presumably lower.

longs   Securities with maturities of twenty years or longer.

M&A   Mergers and acquisitions. M&A departments in investment banks and in some commercial banks help corporate clients formulate and carry out plans for buying or selling other companies or operating units. They also advise on different strategies in hostile takeover situations.

make a market   When a broker takes a position in a security, holding it in the firm's *portfolio* rather than just matching buyers up with sellers.

market   The stock market, usually the New York Stock Exchange.

maturity   The date when a *security* comes due and any outstanding interest and principal must be paid in full.

merchant bank   A bank that can provide both investment banking and commercial banking services. In Europe, merchant banks are legal, but in the United States they technically aren't because of *Glass-Steagall*. Many commercial banks, however, have carefully sidestepped this distinction and are now modeling themselves after the merchant bank concept.

middle market   Companies that do not make the *Fortune 1,000* list, but that aren't "mom and pop" operations either. Sales are usually above $50 million and below $250 million.

money market   The market in which short-term securities are bought and sold. Money market rates refer to short-term borrowing rates. Money market instruments mature in less than one year.

money supply   A measurement used by the *Fed* as one indication of the nation's economic status. Money supply is the stock of money in the economy—specifically, currency and demand deposits at commercial banks.

Moody's   One of the major independent rating agencies of securities.

Munis   Municipal *bonds* issued by state or local governments and their agencies. Munis offer tax-free yields.

number-crunching The sometimes tedious task of preparing and analyzing financial statements, with the help of either a calculator or personal computer.

options An instrument that gives the holder the right to either buy or sell a security at a previously agreed-upon price.

P&L Profit and loss sheet. The income statement of an enterprise.

partnership The most sought-after position in accounting and investment banking firms. Partners are the senior members of the firm and share handsomely in the firm's profits.

PE (P/E ratio) Price-to-earnings ratio. The price per share divided by earnings per share, a formula used by market watchers to determine at what price it makes sense to buy a *stock* on the basis of projected earnings.

platform officers In commercial banking, an *account officer* who has contact with customers of the bank. In the old days of branch banking, loan officers would sit in the back of the bank on a raised platform that was separate from the transactional operations of the teller lines.

pool In investment banking, a work group, usually consisting of junior people, whose members rotate among divisions or who are on call for a number of different areas. Also called a bullpen.

portfolio A collection of investments held by an individual or a corporation.

primary company The insurance company which initially writes a policy that is later syndicated out through reinsurers.

private placement In banking and insurance, putting up funds for a company that wants to raise money but that can't get it in the public market because of cost considerations or an unknown name or credit standing. The company then pays back the interest and principal according to a predetermined schedule. Private placements do not have to be registered with the *SEC*.

pro formas   Projected financial statements

property   A type of insurance designed to protect against property damage.

prospecting   Same as making a *cold call.*

prospectus   A document that describes a securities issue or loan offering, discusses the company, and outlines the terms of the issue.

put   An *option* to sell a security at a given price on a specified date. Opposite of a *call.*

registered rep (RR)   Registered representative. A person registered with the *SEC* to buy and sell securities for customers. One must pass the *Series Seven* exam to become a registered rep.

reinsurance   In insurance, ceding risk to another insurance company (the "reinsurer") at a premium.

relationship banking   A strategy employed in commercial and investment banks to develop a long-lasting relationship with customers over time in the hopes of increasing their loyalty to the bank. Opposite of *transactional banking.*

ROA   Return on assets. The simple but very important ratio of earnings to assets. ROA has become a popular measurement of commercial bank performance.

ROE   Return on *equity.* Ratio of earnings to equity. *ROA* is a function of ROE and *leverage* (debt to equity). A very important measurement of corporate performance, ROE shows how much stockholders are making on their investment.

S&P   Standard and Poor's. One of the most widely followed rating agencies of securities.

S&P 500   A broadly based index of 500 stocks traded on the New York Stock Exchange.

SEC   Securities and Exchange Commission, watchdog of the securities industry. For instance, the SEC makes sure that all information in a *prospectus* reflects the true condition of the company and is not misleading to the public.

security   Any document, whether *stock* or *bond,* that identifies legal ownership or a claim for indebtedness.

Series Seven   The certification exam taken to become a *registered representative* in investment banking.

shelf registration   Registering only once with the *SEC* for all the securities a company wishes to issue over a two-year period. Then, each time the company wants to "go to market" (get money), it simply takes a part of the issue "off the shelf"—instead of registering again with the SEC. The merits and demerits of shelf registration have been a very controversial issue in the securities industry.

short   Selling a security for future delivery in anticipation of being able to buy it cheaper. Opposite of being *long*.

shorts   Securities with maturities of four years or less.

special bracket   The top tier of investment banks—traditionally represented by First Boston, Merrill Lynch, Morgan Stanley, Salomon Brothers, and Goldman Sachs.

spread sheets   Manual or computerized presentations of financial statements. To "spread financials" is to put them in a format that can be used for analytical purposes.

stock   A certificate representing partial ownership of an enterprise, as opposed to a *bond,* which implies a debtor–creditor relationship.

The Street   Wall Street. Used as a general term for investment banks, brokerage firms, and individuals whose field of expertise is *the market.*

T-bills   U.S. Treasury bills. Short-term money market instruments auctioned weekly by the federal government.

tenor   Maturity of debt obligation. A five-year bond has a tenor of five years.

tombstone   An announcement made in financial periodicals regarding a new issue. Such an ad is a matter of public record and is placed by the underwriters and/or advisers of the issue.

transactional banking   A strategy employed by some commercial and investment banks to bid on deals individually instead of developing a special relationship with a company. Opposite of *relationship banking*.

underwriting   The process whereby an investment bank, or syndicate of investment banks, purchases an issue of debt or *equity* from a company and resells it to investors. Also used in the insurance industry with certain insurance policies.

Value Line (Value Line Investment Survey) A weekly listing of various publicly traded companies and opinions regarding their stock prospects in the coming months. A very good, but expensive, source of information for interviewees as well as investors. Available at any library.

venture capital Money invested in start-up companies. Often called seed money.

windows Windows on the market. An outstanding opportunity that occasionally arises in *equity* and debt markers permitting cheaper financing for companies.

Index